# Epitaphs for the Journey

Paul Mariani

# Epitaphs for the Journey:

*New, Selected, and Revised Poems*

Engravings and Design by Barry Moser

Cascade Books ❦ Eugene, Oregon ❦ MMXII

EPITAPHS FOR THE JOURNEY
*New, Selected, and Revised Poems*

*Cascade Books*
*An Imprint of Wipf and Stock Publishers*
*199 W. 8th Avenue, Suite 3, Eugene, Oregon 97401*
*www.wipfandstock.com*
*ISBN 13: 978-1-62032-191-1*

*Cataloging-in-Publication data*
*Mariani, Paul L.*
*Epitaphs for the Journey: New, Selected and Revised Poems. Paul Mariani.*
*The Poiema Poetry Series.*
*p. 23 cm.*
*ISBN: 978-1-62032-191-1*
*PS3563. A6543.E11.2012*
*Made in the U.S.A.*

For Eileen

*Always*

# THE POIEMA POETRY SERIES

Poems are windows into worlds; windows into beauty, goodness, and truth; windows into understandings that won't twist themselves into tidy dogmatic statements; windows into experiences. We can do more than merely peer into such windows; with a little effort we can fling open the casements, and leap over the sills into the heart of these worlds. We are also led into familiar places of hurt, confusion, and disappointment, but we arrive in the poet's company. Poetry is a partnership between poet and reader, seeking together to gain something of value—to get at something important.

Ephesians 2:10 says, "We are God's workmanship . . ." poiema in Greek—the thing that has been made, the masterpiece, the poem. The Poiema Poetry Series presents the work of gifted poets who take Christian faith seriously, and demonstrate in whose image we have been made through their creativity and craftsmanship.

These poets are recent participants in the ancient tradition of David, Asaph, Isaiah, and John the Revelator. The thread can be followed through the centuries—through the diverse poetic visions of Dante, Bernard of Clairvaux, Donne, Herbert, Milton, Hopkins, Eliot, R.S. Thomas, and Denise Levertov—down to the poet whose work is in your hand. With the selection of this volume you are entering this enduring tradition, and as a reader contributing to it.

—D.S. MARTIN
Series Editor

### Other Books in the Series:

SYDNEY LEA, *Six Sundays Toward a Seventh*

ROBERT SIEGEL, *Within This Tree of Bones* (forthcoming)

# CONTENTS

## ONE

## TWO

## THREE

## FIVE

## SIX

## SEVEN

# ONE

# Mairzy Doats

Rewind, Recording Angel, and play again the roll
and rise of Mairzy Doats, the lilt and lift
of those honeyed voices soothing to a small boy
in the back seat listening. The Andrews Sisters
and *doesy doats*, the whole harmonium of bird notes
floating from the radio of my father's all-black
pre-War Ford those sixty years ago. They make
no sense, the syllables that sing *liddle lambsey divey*.
And yet, Angel, how they terrify and comfort.

Behind the wheel, my father's laughing at something
his brother, riding shotgun, a cigarette clenched
between his gleaming teeth, has said. They're making jokes
of words, which I can no more understand than the song
the trinity of sisters sing. Down the wobbling vortex
of memory the wheels go round and round, bumping
over New York's ancient cobbled streets. From above:
the latticed gaps of the Third Avenue El as shuddered
sunlight flickers. Where we've gone or where we're going
I cannot tell. Nor can I now recall a word of what
they said then, Angel, though you know that I was there.
Only splintered sound sloughing on the summer air
and laughter, like a shattered symphony forming
and reforming. Paul to the left and Louie to the right,

those two whose names I carry with me everywhere
I go, names by which the self is fated to be blessed
and cursed, recalled by flickers, if at all:
three bird notes by which the soul is summoned.

Mares eat oats and does eat oats and little lambs
eat ivy. The nursling music reconfigures to reveal
at last a meaning for the boy, which tells him only
this: that the animals were hungry and have been fed.
Up front, there's that mix of English and Italian
laced with French, the odd patois their parents
brought with them when they left Compiano.
And now, in memory's rearview mirror, after all
this time, I catch my father's beseeching eyes dart
in my direction from death's shadows, while Louis
*sesanta anni fa* turns towards me, as if
to let me in on something he's just said.
But there's too much clack and static, as now
his head falls back on his pillow in the casket. . . .

That's it. That's all I can recover: the flecked film
frozen in blacks and whites and sepias, like some
Roman ruin crumbling on a darkling plain, over
which the waves of time are lashing. Two
shadows only, caught on this cloudy moonlit
midnight here by the cold July Atlantic,
like the changing light of that overarching El,
and I alone left to tell this story in which
their names are entered, these two who follow me

everywhere I go, answering still, as mares and does
and lambs answer when they're called, by force
of awe or fear or love or hunger, hoping
to be fed. Oh yes, Angel, hoping to be fed.

## The Lost Father

About Herodotus there is a kind
of reliability, as when he tells
the story of the phoenix, heard
no doubt firsthand, how
the offspring will lug the father

in a ball of myrrh across the sea,
commit them all to flames, to rise
itself renewed, and all its red-gold
feathers dipped with dew. He tells
the story as he says he heard it,

though he is quick to add: I myself
have never seen him. . . .
This pocket watch is at least
sixty years old, so the squint-eyed
jeweler up in Turners told me

when I brought the pieces in
for him to put together. After
forty years mummy-wrapped in faded
tissue, of course the guts were rusted.
But it was all she'd somehow kept

enough intact to pass over from
her father to her son. "He was standing
in his robe," she said, "one hand
on the doorjamb, while the other
rubbed his chest. *Tell your*

*mother to come here a second.* I stopped
playing with my doll when I saw him
wince like that and did what I was
told. Soon there was the white
ambulance. It was the last I ever

saw him, that is, alive." Build us
a story out of that one: Jersey Pollack
on the trail after the elusive Pancho
Villa at 17, then a year later
gassed in some French trench.

Trucking entrepreneur in small-town
Singac, burning down with Bright's,
then dead at thirty-three. In one
of the few photos I have of him, he's cut
his own head off, so that we may better see

Red his stallion, army issue, like his saddle
carbine. Then posing on his Harley,
then with his daughter and his wife.
But to hear his old watch tick again
clink clunk clink clunk, reassembled

like the limbs of some Egyptian god,
the cold bright brass nested against
my ear, as often he must have done—
this gives comfort. In less time
than it takes the second hand to jerk

from one line to the next, his bright
eye winks at my frightened mother.
He is trying to console her, as I know
he must have done, though I should
add, I myself have never seen him.


## Operating Room, Upper East Side, March 1945

Those wooden floors with their pine-scented antiseptic
and the argus-eyed lights in the gunmetal shadows
of the 59th Street Bridge. And there you are, a small boy

strapped to a gurney as the mask covers your face,
the sweet smell muffling your cries, two nurses in white
guiding you down some endless hall, the click of wheels

going round & round. And your younger brother tied
to the table beside you, still and unmoving, as if already
lost, and the ether takes hold and the body goes under.

The body unfolds & the music begins, much as a mother's
musings, the missing mother who went off through
the locked door, whispering *it's all right, it's all right,*

*my little ones, you'll be fine, fine, just fine-O.* And you listen
in the time you have left to the honeyed humming
in the spinning brain, the merest medley of song, so that

even the glint of that scalpel becomes part of the song now,
as the mother sings on, bending above you, bidding
her pretty ones to let go as she has and give over to sleep.

## The Furnace: July 1945

Now, at three in the morning, the old
furnace under the oak floor chuffs furiously,
until the bed itself begins to tremble....

I sit on the tub's edge, feet dangling
in the summer air, a cockroach skittering
under the cast-iron lion's paw

as now the droning begins to flood the flat,
shaking the windowpanes, until I cry out,
my father shouldering through to see

what in God's name is grounding up the air
with that drowning sound. And now
he lifts me to look out the bathroom window

five flights up. Above: flying in sharp
diagonals from left to right over lower
New York City, trinities of bombers, ponderous

metal bees droning toward the west, hundreds
on hundreds on hundreds of them, until the door
and floor and walls and I are shaking. Bombers,

ours, fresh from Europe, and bound now
for Japan, before Truman opted for those
instant suns instead. It was years before

I understood the virtues of the bomb
and recognized the strategic use
of fireballing population centers like London,

Dresden, and Nagasaki. I was five then, and
have no other memory of the war but that:
the drumming sound that shook the very house,

when my father, still in his army uniform,
placed his strong palm upon my head
as if to comfort. He was twenty-eight, and

laughing at his uncomprehending son,
even as the heavens darkened with those
avenging angels he kept telling me were friends.

## Christmas Eve 1945

They've propped me with a comforter
there in the living room just off the dim-lit kitchen,
where reddish bubble lights keep winking
from the etched-out blue black spruce. The scratched

mahogany top of Uncle Charlie's secondhand
Dumont lies pried open at an angle like some coffin
lid, flickering gray images off its five-inch screen.
I'm five, alone, enmeshed now in the first TV

pictures I've ever seen, the strains of a violin
playing klezmer music as Army bulldozers nose
white manikins forward, legs and arms flailing
as they tumble headlong into the pit. A pall

of snow pitches forward into the darkness
of these tenements as a voice keens there
from the console, though it's the music I keep hearing,
notes long since tattooed upon my tattered brain.

For the thousandth time the Army bulldozers
turn again, nosing the bodies forward into the waiting
maw. Once more the dark night the Psalmist sang of
hunkers down, as if keeping watch, except that

they're all gone now, the once-living and the dead, returned
now to the depths from which we all once sprang. Nothing
for it then, old cantor, but to sing them on their way, all those
with names, names only, and the million nameless ones.


## Fathers & Sons

The boy sits on the edge of the iron bed, both
feet inches off the floor, rocking back & forth,
forth & back, clutching the brown paper bag
containing his clean socks & his hairbrush,
as he watches the slant tick tock of sunlight
inch over the floorboards, the blue shadows
growing long & longer as they darken the twin

rows of beds, and the streetlights at long last blink on.
Like the wise virgin in the story, he keeps watch
for his father, while the nice woman smiles her smile,
leaving, then coming back, leaving and coming back, trying
to coax him out of the coat he's buttoned to his neck.
Out in the yard, his close-cropped little brother stalks
the iron-spiked fence, back & forth, forth & back,

once running after a man on the other side he thinks
may be his father, but isn't. In the dark interstices
of this Thanksgiving night, defeated at the last, when
the lamps have all gone out & still the king fails
to appear, the boy on the bed is led downstairs to his brother
& the other lost boys & girls there in the dining room hall
for turkey & turnips & to sing praises to the Lord.

Fast forward fifty Thanksgivings now, and here
they are again: the once-divorced, then twice-widowed
father with his two fast-graying sons, along with
their wives & own grown sons & one babbling grandbaby
there at the table, and three kinds of wine & a hearty meal,
as he likes to say, fit for a king. But a lost king, who came
years late to pick up his kids, and sweep them into his Ford

& wave adieux to the redbrick orphanage somewhere in the Bronx,
then bought them both an ice cream by the 59th Street Bridge
(any flavor they desired), but never told them, then or thereafter,
what kept him from coming for them, and who can't
for the love of God remember now what happened,
or why younger son seems to see right through him,
while the other can't seem to see him right enough.

# New York, Christmas Eve, 1947

Snow falling darkly through darkening air.
Clip-clop of hooves on the cobbles below.
And the Third Avenue El, which will soon disappear.

Cries from the kitchen, cries everywhere.
A boy staring out into darkness below,
and snow falling darkly through darkening air.

Strains of White Christmas on the mothering air.
Winking lights, tinsel, toys, trains, mistletoe.
All, like the El, which will soon disappear.

Under the tree, in the reddish-blue glare,
a father lays train tracks in cottony snow,
while outside snow falls through darkening air.

So much to do, the father's hands say. So much to care
for, so much to fix. And *oh* cries the boy, and *oh*
cries the little toy train, which will soon disappear.

And *oh*, cries the mother, in the kitchen somewhere,
though the boy knows no one is crying. And the snow
goes on falling through the darkening air,
on the stones and the El, which will soon disappear.

# Show & Tell

This poem is for you, Miss B, my once-upon-
a-time 4th-grade teacher, whom I shall never
*never* forget. Back in the fall of '49,
while the invincible Yankees, golden then as ever,

were beating the worthy (but vincible) Red Sox
on the greensward enclosure the late Bart
Giamatti called our New World Paradise,
back when the Russians ended our short-

lived hegemony created by those twin
phoenixes rising sublimely over Hiroshima
and Nagasaki, thus ending our so-called invincibility
with their H-bomb, and that a monster,

at that very moment, Levittown, Long Island
(ex-potato-farm & homemade muddy Eden
for all those GIs like my father) was still so new
it didn't even have a school it could call its own.

The answer was to bus us kids across the tracks
to picturesque Old Bethpage, replete with its oaks
& maples out of Norman Rockwell. Flame red
the leaves, I remember them, and, yes, bright gold.

With every step I took across those ancient wooden floors
my imitation leather shoes would squeak. And when
at last my sad pants split up the back, you gathered
three other ladies, teachers like yourself, then

told me to bend over in the courtyard to pick up stones,
my backside showing through the tear, much, ah!
*much* to your delight, Miss B, until one teacher
finally had the decency to call the torture

to a halt. And now that I am twice the age
you were back then. Miss B, now, before the bell
dismisses both of us for good, I want to thank you,
especially for the morning ritual of Show & Tell.

Everyone did Show & Tell, you reassured me.
Everyone. Tomorrow it would be *my* turn, you said,
to present my Show & Tell. I worked hard that night,
sweating a cold sweat to try & make a decent card.

Scissors, ribbons, old crayons, colored paper. The whole
shebang, you know. Except we had no tape or glue
at home, and certainly no money then, for either
tape or glue. I even tried to make a home brew

of flour mixed with water, but the batter
wouldn't stick. Nothing stuck. finally, I sewed
the goddamn thing together & made a card for you:
a red heart rampant  on a piece of yellowed board,

which, Miss B, you held at arm's length
between your thumb & finger, away from you,
and, before that class of strangers, asked why,
instead of sewing it, I hadn't simply glued

the thing together, the way *any* of the other
children would have done. I said nothing then,
or when I had to take the children's jeers
down on the playing field that noon, or even when

I got back home and hid, or at any time since then.
Except, Miss B, the kid grew up the way
kids do. In time, the boy from the other side
of town learned to read & write & say

things proper-like, and make a proper bow.
And now, Miss B, though you may already be in hell
& I left speaking to a ghost, I have come back to try
to get it right this time. Miss B, this is *my* Show & Tell.


## Duet

Noon: the Jones Beach causeway
shimmering in the August haze,
the hoods of overheated Fords
& Packards, Depression black, and by
the thousands, stalled in traffic.
My brother, sister & myself in back,
my mother with the baby on her lap
up front, my father inching forward
as if still testing Shermans

for the Army. She tried to salvage
things by turning up the radio
to sing, my mother, for she sang
beautifully, and she was beautiful
and young. She kept coaxing him
to sing along with her, her bell-bright
voice & his in harmony. A duet.
Bass & alto. The male & female of it.
But there he was, my father, leaning
on his horn as someone
tried to inch around him. Then that someone
shouting through my father's window,
my mother pleading, my father out
the door, then back & vindicated. . . .

Forty years, forty years, and still
I see her, her lips pale and shaken
in the rearview mirror as we sat there
stunned & silent. By then the music
on the radio was gone. Gone too
whatever song she had been singing,
ground down again first to a sound
like bearings scraping, then tears,
then after that to nothing.

# Goodnight Irene

I am ten and a half and my father
has let me come to work with him again
at Scotty's Esso in Mineola, the wood
and plaster Tudor building three blocks
east of the pseudo-Bauhaus boy's
Catholic highschool, from which one day
I will venture out to try the priesthood on
(and fail) knowing it is not
for me when I start keeping (against
Brother Clyde's injunction) a marker
in my physics textbook beside the picture
of the lovely in the arm-length cashmere sweater
with those swelling upturned breasts.

And from beneath the row of fan belts
hanging spiderlike I can see the neon
Rheingold sign pulse dully in the doorway
of the Colonial Bar & Grill
where thirteen years from now Wilbur
will split my upper lip with an ice cube
flung across the smoky underwater room
before my brother Walter can hit him
easy with that cross-body block of his
while I reel off my drunky speech to these
my friends a week before my marriage.

But for now I am inside the station
listening to my father singing chorus
after chorus of "Irene, goodnight, Irene,
I'll see you in my dreams," seeing only
part of his face down in the grease pit,
the wrench in his clenched right fist,
his hooded lamp throwing fitful shadows
all across the wall, as he performs
whatever mysteries it is he does to cars.

Useless even to my father, I watch
the yellow sunlight blocked in squares
drift east across the blackened bench
where two half-moon brake drums cup
the ballpeen hammer as in a Juan Gris
still life, the calendar (gift of *Kelly's
Tires*) still turned to August, above which
the cellophane with the nightie
painted on it conceals the underlying
mystery of the lady kneeling there
who smiles frankly at me.

And now the warm smell of leaking
kerosene from the thumb-smeared
darkgreen fifty-gallon tin as I wipe
the opaque bottles of reconstituted oil
for the old *"baraccas"* as my father calls them.

On the box radio above the wheezy
Coke machine, word drones
Marines are fighting in a place
called Seoul but there is trouble even
closer home and soon someone is singing
once again the song my father
also loves to sing, "Irene, Goodnight."

And I think of mother back in Levittown
teaching Walter how to read
as my sisters go on playing dolly,
the younger one putting her wedding dress
on backward while I help my father
put all the bolts into one coffee can
and all the nuts into the other.

And now my Uncle Vic (the one
the strokes choked off three years ago)
grabs his grease-clogged rag
and mutters as he strides out
into the sun to gas up some revved-up Ford,
the static gurgling high above the engine's
macho rumble while my father goes on working
on the underbelly of the car
where the light is coming from,
singing yet again "Goodnight, Irene."

But my mother's name is not Irene
her name is Harriet and I wonder why

my father wants to see this other lady

in his dreams but I cannot ask
and will not even know what it is
I want to ask until I am older
than he is this September afternoon in 1950
and now the tears well up for him
and for my mother and myself as I turn
to look back down into the empty pit
to tell him now I understand.


## Study in Black & White, 1954

Seven days a week, six till ten,
my father & I ran the Sinclair station
across from the county courthouse in Mineola.
Between customers I pored over *The Greatest
Story Ever Told* and *Amboy Dukes*

or worked out back among the jewelweed
& cinders, swabbing ball bearings in kerosene,
as I gloried in all I would in time become.
Late April, early May. The trees trembling
for the sun's caress. Hummed the papers

daily now of the noose grown tighter
round Dien Bien Phu. Black & white photos,
ghostly, dreamlike, with black-pajammed Viet
Minh sappers storming trenches, as elite
French paratroopers, bloodied, dazed, surrendered.

I was fourteen & stood ready
to take on evil wherever it reared
its swollen head, like the Archangel Michael
whose eight-foot statue hovered high above
the marble-white gothic altar of Corpus Christi,

armored like the boy god Augustus Imperator,
his bronze spear stirring the snarling serpent.
Only Butch, who lived behind the diner
two doors down in his '41 wood-trimmed Chevy
wagon up on blocks, cared nothing

that the world my G.I. father had helped
make safe was once more breaking down.
Butch spent himself poring over comics,
small ones, black & white, in which Wimpy did
forbidden things to Olive. In all weathers,

buried beneath a filthy army-issue blanket
flanked by whisky flasks & yellow newsprint,
his palsied body shook. But who knew anything
about Butch really? Where he came from or later
where he went? My father warned me away from him,

and when I asked why, he simply stared at me
in utter disbelief. Could any son of his
be that goddamned stupid & still walk upright
the face of God's sweet earth? That was forty
years ago, so that by now Butch has surely

returned to the same dust from which
we all once sprang, his end coming in some alley,
or one fine morning not waking from the backseat
of his wagon, monoxide leaking into his final
dream of love to resurface here defanged:

thinning hair slicked back, the toothless grin,
the right hand grasping the palsied left
to hide the shaking as he sized you up, a face
you'd recognize in any bathroom mirror,
the poor forked mortal trembling thing itself.

## Matadero, Riley & Company

The one circling the other like a jackal,
hackles bristling, his left fist feinting first
then jabbing at the bloodied face,
playing him like a cat clawing
at his wounded prey. I watched
from the safety of my front lawn,

staring at the ring of boys
expanding and contracting
Only the crack of Riley's fists against
Matadero's face broke the eerie silence.

I would make more sense of all
of this, but the names are gone,
even from the black-and-white
Kodak shots I have of them,
though one's a cop they say
out on the Island and another
sells sneakers down in Tampa,
and one did time for breaking
someone's neck in a barroom down
in Merrick, and two at least are dead.
Most are married now (and half of them
divorced) with teenage children of
their own: working-class stiffs
who bought the dream without
the substance—myself among them—
the wops, the poles, the micks
giving way with time to
Rodriguez, Alicea, and Rivera.

A shadow world only, though
the scars still itch. Matadero,
waiting for me as I clambered
up the far steps of the piss-soaked
tunnel that ran beneath the railroad

tracks. How I used to pray for him
to die. At least to be delivered
from his grip. And now Riley,
catching up at last with my tormentor,
jabbing at his face, again, again.
Cat-and-mouse, a jab, jab
and then another, while Matadero's arms
hung, too bone-weary to keep the blows
from landing on his disfigured face.
On that cold March morning thirty years
ago, while the clouds drifted piecemeal
overhead, the age of Riley replaced
the short-lived age of Matadero.
For months after Riley and company
pursued the beaten loser. Even I
walked about with something like
impunity. But in the waste of time it all
comes down again to *Ecce Homo*.
Behold: one more human being beaten,
this one on the playing fields of Mineola.

# TWO

## East of the Whitestone

Where the East River fuses with the Sound
we rowed furiously against the waves,
Bob and I, and a third whose name I think
was Burns. We were fifteen then, and the talk
was girls, and this our first sorry venture
into the fierce Sublime, though it must
have looked from the Whitestone as if we were
merely fishing east of the Throgs Neck.
Cold, salt, dark, unplumbed, and unforgiving
the river. And there was Bob, working his oar
while the waves grappled with the flimsy gunwales.
And there's the yellow letter I found up in the attic
that tells me Burns was there, though
for the love of me I can't remember him. And I was
there, the one addressing you, who is also slowly
disappearing. But in the spring of '55 it was I
who pulled the second oar for all our lives.

For nearly thirty years I lost touch with Bob
and do not believe I will see Burns again this side
of Stygia. Bob lives in California now, with his
wife and two grown daughters. And Bob's grown
rich, though he pointed to a suit and beard
he said could buy and sell him ten times over.
Back then we rowed to stay alive, joking weakly
of girls and God knows what as the storm kept
coming on, until it seemed the boat would swamp

in those unforgiving cold crosscurrents. And if it had,
there'd be no question now of who was or wasn't in the boat,
or who made it, in any sense you care to take those words.

And though we caught nothing but a single eel
which then we hacked to death as a scapegoat offering,
the river gods at last relented to leave us on the dusty
farther shore. As for Burns, I hope he has a wife and kids
and has somehow managed to stay afloat, unlike
so many other friends whom I could mention.
Afterwards, we paid the boatman and walked
back down the street to Bob's, talking of how brave
we were, and of what we'd eat for dinner, and what
we'd do that night, and would the Whitestone girls be there.


## The Sweater

Loomed my first real Saturday night date.
My father winked & beamed as he led me
into the master bedroom, where he unstuck
the bottom drawer of his highboy dresser
to bestow on me, his firstborn—about

to be initiated into the mysterious, head-spinning,
perfumed world of women—his Sunday-best
imitation cashmere sweater. His eyes glazed
with memories of his own lost youth
even as he spoke. He still had half a foot

and half a hundred pounds on me, but if
I flexed both my biceps, and kept my shoulders
rigor mortis stiff, and if I sucked in air in a sort
of blowfish style I just might make the sweater fit.
This was it, he whistled: my bestowment,

bar mitzvah, confirmation, manhood's
yummy threshold & inner sanctum moment.
I was just sixteen, and so (alas) would need
either to take three buses or be driven
by my father in the family's green two-toned

Pontiac to the other side of town
to retrieve my beautiful blue-eyed blonde
with her Cinderella curls and wide smile,
who seemed bathed in some unearthly light
and who had inexplicably said yes (yes!)

when I'd asked her out to see Charlton (Moses)
Heston take out Pharaoh's boys & all his horses.
Came sage advice with my father's sweater.
Shake the father's hand, he said. Be firm,
but don't try to grind his knuckles. Sweet talk

the mother, yes this, yes that, and, as for
the girl: laugh at all her little jokes, walk
on the outside, & be careful not to let her
catch you staring down her blouse. Above all,
be a gentleman. My mother, who'd heard it all

before, rolled her eyes & groaned. She, who'd
heard all the stuff Mister Wonderful was dishing
out, had her own advice to offer. Treat her the way
you would your mother or your sister's friends.
Have fun, and remember how lucky *any* girl would be

to be going out with *my* smart, handsome son.
And so, decked out in my father's sweater,
the looming night proceeded to unloom.
A sweet time, too, it was, & lyrical & poignant,
& very nearly a success, except that, by the time

we left Moses & the movie, the Fates had sent
the Red Sea up our way, backing up along
the sidewalks while we waited on the corner
for my father, who showed up two hours late
to take me & my half-drowned Cinderella home.

And that was that. And though I never dated
her again, I still remember her enigmatic smile (ah yes),
and hope she's blessed, as I have been, and—even better--
doles out wisdom sounder than I got when I gave
my father back his ruined imitation cashmere sweater.

# Work

And so it went, day after day, the four of us, inching
out from the shallow end of the empty Empire
Swimming Pool, the ritual of gearing up to sandblast,
preparing to engorge our peck's worth of aqua metal dust.
Worse was the glare off the rain-scum slop congealing
at the deep end, the sun's reflection blinding us whenever
we looked back. In silence I pushed on, without even
Bo Diddley's music or the King's to ease me through my hell.

My father seemed bent on getting a day's work out of
each of us even if it killed us and the sun didn't beat him
to the punch. By week's end it was making good on that
promise as we brushed the pool a second coat of blue.
Florida Blue, Bay of Naples Sheen, Cote d'Azur, the veriest
blue of blue, that would transform fifteen thousand gallons
of chlorine-threaded water so that 700 day camp kids
might plash about, squealing in that too too happy summer
soon to come. Meanwhile there were cabins to Lysol-rinse,
two palominos to quarter (illegally) on the abutting
state preserve, and Rusty the Little Choo-Choo to set
chugging once again along the western chainlink fence
patrolled each dusk by the boss's German Shepherds.

Come September, I would hie me off to the fall-gold hills
of Beacon Prep, where I would rise each morning to chant
a version of the Office, then struggle with my fourth-year
Latin, singing of the epic birth of the world that flourished

once on the Tiber's sullen banks. But for now that world
beckoned as oasis only. Here, inside this blazing pit ruled silence,
punctuated by the bark of orders from a man who had a pool
to finish, blood-thick paint baking the metal and our hands
under that Egyptian sun, while darkened each day more
my princely skin. Sunt lacrimae rerum. Prisons are a state
of mind. Oases ditto. Somewhere, I'd heard, shone words
and plashing water. A lake, a rope, a letting go. Somewhere too
a plunging downward, then bubbles rising slowly to the top.


## The Girl Who Learned to Sing in Crow

Plash of water from the kitchen sink, a spotless
blue sky eastering through the open window
above the gleaming faucet, and a fistful of buttercups
plucked by their tender stems from along

the border of our rusting fence, placed just so
along the white formica sill as if framed.
An image of my sister's still life—*nature
morte*—as once more the mind's eye

catches her washing a heap of dishes
like the little mother she used to think she was,
as she sang softly to herself, like some blind
canary that sings because it must. Ah,

how she sang with all the bright abandon
of her tender years, long and softly, though her brothers,
not knowing what to make of such graceful notes,
mocked and mimicked her with counter song, *caw*! *caw*!

No need now to rehearse the pressures there
to stun and stunt a voice. The truth is that
even now I cannot bring myself to say it all.
Call it the pockmarked havoc of our growing up.

Call it whatever name you bloody please.
It's all behind us, we tell ourselves. And who wants
to take the blame for the silence which says so well
how we treat our women? How we mock them for

the very courage we ourselves gasp after in our locked
and airless rooms. Or sacrifice their hopes to men
stronger than ourselves, slapping back and rump
in winking fellowship, so that, as one day yields

to yet another, we still catch glimpses of a scrawny
girl learning how to split her tongue and caw.
Hell, we know it happens all the time. We know
just as they do it's the song birds make good eating.

## Winter 1956

Stone bridge at Andau
and the brazen soldier, soldier, a
kid as I was then, cocking
his stolen sten machinegun.

NKVD heaped
on the frozen cobblestones
of storied Budapest, white-
limed to help them rot:

*Look's* photographs of the New
Order hung beneath the crucifix
in the old stone study hall
in Beacon, New York....

Two and by two
filing across the yard
through the new dawn snow
along with forty other novices.

Yes, and the little German priest
framed in the chapel light, shaking
as he lifted up the bread and cup,
so much in love with God he was.

Another sixteen years and
we have come full circle.
When I call my kids to supper,
they are still playing guns.

# Photograph of Oldest Son,
# Postulant in the Society of Mary,
### *Taken with Proud Parents at Beacon, New York*

Two men, one forty, the other seventeen....
Both stand stiffly in their Sears & Roebuck suits
in the deckled black & white snapshot,
April 1957. Between them the woman,

aged 34, hollow-cheeked & unsmiling
in her two-piece maternity dress
buttoned at the top, her short hair
rain-bowed by a clip of artificial flowers.

Her body tilts slightly towards her son,
who seems to pull away from her
on his aloof & solitary axis. The son
himself is tall, though not so tall

as his father, whose close-cropped hair
and shoulders dominate the picture.
He has planted his right hand firmly
on his left wrist, exactly like

his father, as the two men stand there
smiling for the camera. Behind them
three trees in the shadow of the rectory
and the flatness of the graywhite sky.

Still, he remembers. He remembers
how his littlest brother, all ears
and straw-stubble hair, eyes
wide, in the cold blue Easter air

shouted the news that they
were gonna have another baby.
He remembers too his mother's look
as she moved step by underwater

step towards the imitation marble
Blessed Mother where he stood waiting
in his Sunday hand-me-downs, knowing
he had been betrayed once more

by the honeyed love of generation,
even as he & his mother & his father
composed themselves before the camera,
each one careful not to touch the other.

## Soldiers of Christ

Mid-winter glare as I drive once around
the granite stone retainer in disbelief.
The school is gone now, the chapel too,
and the playing fields: all gone. Even

the mountain over which the sun rose
and where God would often greet me
has turned to ice and stone. Gone too
that gaggle of German nuns who fed us,

and Brother Frank, who could still smile,
though arthritis had bent him nearly double.
Gone my classmates, every one of them,
from that cold stone dim-lit study hall.

Even the old marching music is gone, which
cheered us on that Memorial Day all those years ago.
And you: you in your Marian blue uniform
with the gold trim, your snare drum dragging

from your waist, you, who at seventeen
stood there in the front ranks of that Catholic
boys' Marching Band on Beacon's Main Street,
that boy gone as well. Six weeks' practice

and the sticks still bent like rubber. And good
Brother Ed, standing in the doorway, cheering
us on in that upstate accent he affected.
"Now boys, some of the local rowdies

are goin' to try and get at you. Don't pay them
no attention. Remember: you are soldiers
of Christ and his blessèd mother, Mary. No tit
for tat; just offer it up and keep on marchin'."

And sure enough, there they were, on the corner
at the hill's crest, the sun high now, so that sweat
began gathering beneath my too-huge Salvation
Army cap, there in their black leather jackets

and motorcycle caps brushed back at a jaunty
angle, toothpicks dangling Brando-like
from the corners of their mouths, the sudden
shock of jeers, catcalls, and the quick flicks

of middle fingers as my hands tensed
and my spine began to tingle. And still we
stumbled on, Christ's soldiers and me
up front drumming, left right, left right

as we marched on toward the beckoning oily
waters of the Hudson, our flag held high, hearts
high and faces forward, left right left, in five
fourths time to the heady music only we could hear.

# Betty: September 1957

And the fumbling. Oh blessed Lord the fumbling,
the sweetness, when the massive etched-in-adamantine
moral Code, self-imposed with spit-polish discipline,
at last began breaking into ice floes, as with Stalin's
bronze imposing too-huge statue pulled down
upon the cobbled streets of Budapest as I had witnessed
the fall before on the twelve-inch black & white
in the refectory there at Beacon, all come crashing down
at last against the warm transmission hump rising
from the floor of Grippie's '53 Ford, where I sat erect,
half kneeling before the plush dark brilliance
of that gardenia softness that curled before me.

Early September, dark & warm, night easing into
Sunday morning, the haloed cicada glow of a humming
streetlight with its scalloped-edged reflector.
And the glowing music on the radio, crooning
"Goodnight Sweetheart, well, I really must go,
goodnight sweeeeeetheart, goodnight,"
the black cathedral-high arched elms awash
with the benediction of the present.

That year, that now-done year at Beacon Prep
with its benzene-bright Sublime, the moiling waters
of Niagara suspended even as they fell, like some
butterfly transcendence impossible to hold. And parked
now, just two streets down from the Catholic highschool

where all the heroic bifurcated tension had begun.
I can still hear Grippie, busy up front negotiating
the clumsy steering wheel with his sweetheart there
beneath him. "Hey, priest," he is saying, "ain't this better
than the stuff they fed you at the Sem? Go on,
quit your agonizing and go ahead & kiss her."

But even I need no prompting for the adoration that
I feel, as my trembling fingers touch in utter disbelief
the throbbing vein along her neck, and then the plumdark
lips uplifted toward me as the silver tinkling tintinnabulation
of the bells, bells, bells begin ringing Easter more sweetly even
than that Angelus we sang by candlelight before the May Day
statue of Our Lady when we crooned our blessed Aves.
Ah, that lovely curve of breast beneath her thin white sweater,
which I vowed there & then ever to defend from violation,
even as I sank my head into her shoulder, praising Him
for the good I'd found here in the midst of so much darkness.
As in that other garden, when clay first rubbed its eyes,
amazed to find that strange & lovely complementary shape
& I came off my earnest, stringent year-long fast
& kissed her lips & dear God tasted woman once again.

*The* Johns Hopkins University,
he let me know, as I staggered
half dizzy from lifting cases
of Campbell's Soup cans by the hour

from off the high-strung metal roller ,
rising from the cellar to greet him
as my father had taught me
to shake the hand of any man who held

his hand out, his rugger's grip
hard enough to granulate my knuckles,
his lips curled up beneath
his steady Anglo-Saxon star blue gaze.

A world of slave and master in the voice
& carriage, something the Third,
the face done a hundred times
by Rockwell Kent: blond & tanned, pure

poster propaganda art. I'd have given
a week's pay to bring a wrench
down on that sullen head, if I thought
I might live to tell the story.

Those long weekday nights at a buck
ten an hour in the Garden City
A&P, shell-shocked balding Arnie,
that Ernie Pyle ex-master sergeant,

lone liberator of some Bologna outhouse.
who ran the motley night crew, hard
and unrelenting, except the few soft nights
he said he had a promise from his wife.

And Winslow, Grand Assistant Manager,
tub in horn-rimmed glasses waddling
with a pepperoni stuck between
his legs, screaming at poor black L. C.,

the best man in that place. L.C.,
old and tired, having seen it all.
"This big, L. C., you got one this big?"
Dumbass Winslow, who tried to fire me

the one time I celebrated, having somehow
passed my impossible Calculus exam,
and drank too much returning from Manhattan
College, blue-collar Irish mostly, and surely no

Johns Hopkins. Still, it was four steps
up from the ninth grade, where
the Depression had balked my parents
and whisked them off to work. Fidel's army

had just taken Havana, like Joe Louis
that second time with Schmeling:
a sudden disestablishment of bankers
& politicos in the *Newsday* sequence

standing blindfold before their shallow
graves, then toppling and disappearing.
So it could be done, I warmed myself
over coffee in the local diner, fuming over

the injustice of it all. My enemy took all
the easy aisles, while the night crew ate it,
knowing he had the bosses' favor. I kept my eye
on the conveyor with its uploading

cardboard cartons, Johns Hopkins's
miserable coffin replayed among the peaches
& spaghetti, consigned him grandly
to the deepest darkness I could then imagine,

& waited, recalling the Oriente outpost
Fidel had failed to take at the beginning,
that abortive, rallying 26th July,
then his prison durance & the amnesty

and handshakes, as the bearded prophet
waited out his time, like that cold & distant star
winking high above the garbage heaped out back,
in darkness waiting as I would have to wait.

## Manhattan

Thirty years, and the six-inch scar still there
like a white & leprous flower. Five beers
& five Manhattans at this college bar
in Hempstead & then south with Peers
& Wilbur to the White Castle as I chatter
on about my Ethics test & how Aquinas avers
means can be said to justify the ends (or
is it ends means?) when they're there,
this one in stud leather who insists on star-
ing at my Manhattan College jacket. And before
I know it, we're out behind the building, under
the springtime stars, both staggering, stud leather
leering & coming at me, until in sheer terror
I tear into him, fists knotted in his greasy hair,
smashing his head against the blacktop border.
And in two minutes it's over, & through a blur
of cheers I'm downing five Manhattans more,
then swimming upstreet through some phosphor glare
to steal a men's sign for some faceless stranger,
ten feet of coiled barbed wire having so far
stopped him.
           But nothing can stop Manhattan, no sir,
and halfway up the pole razor teeth shear
my leg to lace & then I'm down. And when I pare
back an eyelid the morning after, pain is everywhere,
and there's this ugly fish mouth wound down there,
and I'm tearing past my mother, & at 9:05 I glare

at Ethics Question 1, then down at my bloody cor-
duroys & across at Self-loathing & old friend Fear,
both already bored, & yawning at whatever answer
I come up with for Questions 2 & 3 & 4.

## Replaying the Old Morality Play

Before the dull and torpid fire of the large
red book he stared, ear straining for some
hidden music he sensed himself, repelled
by the miasmic fumes, somehow stirring towards.

Long too had the chipped cup of tea sat there
beside him, flanked on either side
by crusts of sodden toast still unconsumed,
his sick head dizzy and his eyes aswim.

The single bulb hummed dully overhead
and the house was still. And the words
kept swimming there before him, like blips
across his fevered brain. Just how long

he had been staring at the text (or was it
merely pre-text?) before he knew for sure
his sister was standing there beside him
like some blanched and wingless Nike

to force him from his reverie, who could say?
At last he too could smell the fumes, seeping in
from the attached garage. Nothing for it then
but once more to rescue his Andromeda, his

desperate mother who had sealed herself
once more behind the driver's seat of their
ancient Pontiac. According to the familiar
ritual she had done it, first closing the coffered door,

then hooking the rear egress, then turning on
the engine and settling back until the fumes
had reached the King his father, rousing him
from his troubled winter's sleep, where he waited,

while his son went out into the eerie darkness
and forced the battered door, a handkerchief
at his nose and mouth, then banged on the misting
windshield where her drowsy locks had come to rest.

How does one assume the proper tone when one's
mother comes that close to this eerie, comic tragedy
played out on a winter's night in a place like Mineola?
To force? to plead? perhaps to joke, cajole? And why him

and why his sister in their bit parts of *Hamlet Redivivus*,
while the King, in grease-stained long johns, waited
in the dim-lit hall for the wretched Queen to make
another comeback? In terror now he banged

upon the windshield, watching for her head
to bob up quick while all about the swirl of chalk-white
clouds kept laughing. At last she stirred and killed
the engine, unlocked the door, and then, as if

lurching underwater, pushed past him, then
staggered up the steps and back inside.
The King, upstaged, could only stare, disarmed
and wordless, before he followed her to bed.

As for the princeling hero of the play? A quaff
of crust and tea as a final consummation,
the book closed up, the hall light doused,
then upstairs to bed. Only his sister's eyes

floating in the sea wrack and his mother's damasked
head remained. Come morning, his book
would still be there to comfort, the noble sentiments
dancing in indifferent splendor down the page.

## Light Streaming Into the Head

When the light trickles through the cracked
panel of my son's closed door at 5:00 a.m.
I know he's at his books again,
the night watchman waiting for his dawn.

Last week, once he'd gulped his oatmeal down
and driven off to school, I waded through
the clutter of his room, looking for his razor.
Among the thumbed stack of Spanish words,
the strange quadratic symbols, the postcard
pictures of the Last Judgment at Autun
and the Parthenon against the pink dawn eastering,
I found his dog-eared paper Bible beside
a blood-stiff crumpled handkerchief, old signs
I too well know of hours spent searching
in a cell-like room for light to come or come
again while waiting for the niggling words
to kindle into flame....
                  I was his age the first time
I think it struck, though I can see how long
it was in coming, the way my highschool physics
textbook showed the motes swarming in the heated air
until at last they coalesced and flamed, charged
as jagged sheets of lightning to leave
the dark forever altered on the stunned mind's eye.
But who at first could have told the difference?
Another day of classes at Manhattan College,
the long drive there in traffic and back again
in twilight autumn drizzle in my buddy's
hearse-gray '57 Ford. Night after night I took my dinner
on the run to make the nightshift at the Garden City
A&P by six, where I stacked Rice Krispies, cans of corn
and apricots along the gaping, hungry rows.

Near midnight I'd be home again, my parents
and the younger six asleep, ready
for another round of wrestling with my books.

But this once, things were different. By 3:00 a.m.,
the coffee sloshing at the bottom of my cup
and the nosebleeds for the moment stanched,
all at once my head went light when Jowett's Plato
gave way to the unexpected music of Ovid's
*Metamorphoses*, the passage where the boyish
husband turns in dark to find his dear wife
gone and calls out into the indifferent
shadows after her: *Eurydice. Eurydice.*
The cry of the bereft. And then, whether it was
the giddy hour or because I felt my heart
leap at once across some barrier of tongues,
which no hell I knew could keep me from,
I felt a light so warm, so very warm and gentle,
like nothing I had ever felt before, like, like
a golden river flooding through my head.

You know of course how all such rivers sink.
And soon you are looking for the answer
in a blood-streaked handkerchief, or too many
cups of coffee, or the metal ticking clock. Time
to hit the sack. I staggered to the bathroom sink
and stared into the surface of the giddy mirror,
then splashed my face and looked again to see

the same gaunt pimply face, the stubbled chin,
the untamed hair still charged and bristling.
Only in the eyes had something changed....
And then the still-fresh memory of Beacon
dying on the sewer-bloated still majestic Hudson:
the town where I'd tried to make myself
into a priest and failed. And yet once I'd felt a light
like this flaring from the puffy, frog-like eyes
of the little German priest whose name
I have forgotten, a gentle, self-effacing presence
whose liver-mottled hands had once brushed light
across the dusty shelves which housed, he said,
his Virgil and his Ovid and that Bunsen flame
Catullus until his eyes had flared, brightening
the dusty room, and I had stared, wondering
where all the light was streaming from.

You wait and then you learn to wait some more.
All you can do is turn each empty page, hungry
for whatever light there is, as you try
to blink back the time when something brilliant
flickered blooming in the head. In the meantime
this: that quickening in my own son's eyes,
a river, light, a hope, a something, as when
Plato's dizzy prisoner, as I once heard,
neck bent and groping backwards from his cell
for air, aware of shadows trailing at his feet,
at last looked up to catch full on his face
the staggering honeyed brilliance of the sun.

# THREE

# Harry

*And, as we hear you do reform yourselves,*
*We will, according to your strengths and qualities,*
*Give you advancement.*

*Henry IV. Part 2.*

The paisley kerchief blooming
from his breast pocket, the greengray
windsor-knotted tie, the chain looped
across the waist, the horn-rimmed glasses.
Harry's impeccable lectures on myne own
Sir Philip Sidney, the Perfect Courtier,
offering his cup of water to the broken
private when he himself lay dying
beneath the arching lowlands tree. Harry,
dead these forty years, striding high then
across the light-laced inner quad,
a French text in his tanned & perfumed hand.
Harry, with the Army Corps of Engineers
on the river at Remagen that late winter
of '45. Were those pearls he strew
before Monahan, McCormick, Walsh, & me
as he lectured on until the very angels
must have wept? Soldier, scholar, statesman,
poet, prince. The very thing itself.

Before the tarnished hallway
mirror, I aped his walk, his talk,
the half-tilt of that aristocratic shoulder.
At last, seeing that even the junk trees
along the fence were breaking into blossom,
I screwed the courage up to ask
for help in going on to grad school.
*"Though I have come late to English, Harry,"*
the words rehearsed for weeks, *"help me,*
*Sir. I give my word I will not let you down."*

And then...and then to watch him turn
away that lovely sculpted head of his
& hear him say it, No. No, How he was sorry,
but he couldn't, no. And then,
but for the intervening half a century
of holding up one's end of the aborted
bargain, that was all. Except to smile
one's embarrassed, crooked smile
& turn away oneself, as on my Harry rushed,
intent on getting where he had to go.

# Crossing Cocytus

## 1

Arc of fire across the black of heaven: a father's fist
in downswing, so that even the sun must avert its gaze.
Midriff, the muscles taut, rib on rib defined, the glint

of honed mahogany, the shock at last acknowledged,
the meaning circling out: cold eccentric pulses
from a probe approaching an erratic world. Jacob,

seeing no way out, confronts the angel there before him,
its pterodactyl windmill wings fanning the dead air
back into motion. To circle, then to lunge, as now your eye

catches his thumbs bent in along the dirt-caked
palms to keep from breaking as they strike.
The muscled neck, black as that oaken corpse

once glimpsed at carnival, organ music piped into
the psychedelic coffin, what had been a woman once,
dredged up from Salt Lake's depths, hawk's talons

going for your eyes, until you smash back these long years later
in an agony of song, your own fist arcing down and over,
the way he taught you, into nose ridge, cheekbone, eye.

**2**

Horn of ibex, horn of goat, a way-down note.
Sounds the self makes in its isolation: grunt,
eructation, breath: the universal given, sustained

by some unseen force even here along the frozen
waters of Cocytus. The bugle sounding at the frozen Yalu
so that we froze in terror, trying to chaff our hands just long

enough to pull our cranky rifles from our blankets
as we waited for the phantoms in the predawn howling wind.
The rabbi there at Belsen: Yom Kippur '44, calling

to his own: a thin cry crushed by the whistle of the train
with its fresh arrivals. Bull's horn, brute force, thick
and dripping between its thighs, brooking no refusal.

The high-rumped gladiator, glaring at whoever dares
oppose him. But, Abba, Father, I too have been given
and so can give. My youngest son, my John, my boy,

eleven, playing scales along his trumpet, the notes
falling and rising with the breath we gave him,
she and I, the instant shattering the imprisoning glass.

Not that, not some goat's head with gargoyle fangs:
dragon, demon, Dracula. Instead, light gathering
to itself, like as when one starts from some troubled sleep,

the thing at first refusing to reveal itself more fully.
As when Jacob, with the first hint of dawn, after struggling
through the drugged hours with the angel, feels the wind shift

and charges the heart be kinder to itself.  As on that morning,
in the first light of a late March dawn, when we walked apart,
though we were none of us alone, and the road revealed itself

ascending, and we heard the grosbeaks and the sparrows,
a cry, a song, a signal, and knew they ushered in the sun.
Remember the comic strips you read back in the 40's?

Joe Palooka's sidekick, Knobby Walsh, morphed from Stepin
Fetchit black to grey to white with the passing years.
The Katzenjammer Kids? Biff boom, bam! Batman and the Japs?

The bathroom mirror at three a.m., when the shadow trembles
in the ether though you stand stock still, until at last you
recognize the stranger, his crow's eyes glaring at you in the glass?

# 4

And one, shivering with the wintry drizzle in that dank trench,
lifting his head now to meet my unsteady gaze. "What,
are you here, too," I asked him (though he was not). His eyes burned

like dying embers, though his cheeks were streaked with tears.
"Hard it is to ask forgiveness, even now," I thought I heard him say.
"My son, listen to what I have to say. I would forget the past and all

we suffered, though we will take it with us into death.
As at the dinner table, when I broke my fist against your face,
there where nose ridge, cheekbone and right eye meet,

and had to wear the sling all summer long, and all because
the words had failed me. Forgive my bastard anger, but when
you answered back you challenged me, your words cutting

below my waist, so that I struck out as I had once taught you."
And I: "Call it the necessary crossing, for I might have parried
at least by cringing back, but chose to take the blow, for I am

my father's son. I have my own sons now who have known
unreasoning anger. That gray-haired older man, potbellied
and hard of hearing, who put his arms about me weeping

when his sister died is not like the other one we knew. Strange
to find you here in my private hell, where I thought to find
myself." And, as I lifted him to kiss his forehead, I heard him say,

"Perhaps, my son, you have." To which I stuttered, wordless,
trying to hold him for a moment longer, even as he faded
at the sounding of a horn, like ice dissolving in the sun.

## 5

For years now haunted by the boy under the great-limbed
purple beech that fronts our home, his scrawny arms
locked about his knees, as he keeps sobbing to himself.

When I call to him he does not answer, as if he could not hear.
He is laced with the gold hush that beech leaves hold
in early spring before they turn to purple like the rest of us.

Strange how his sobbing sounds like singing.
I would comfort him for his having fathered me.
It has come out well, I would have him hear.

I have three sons now myself, my wife, my friends, my God.
And I have even learned to sing, though it sound more like
the caw of crow. I see now that you raised me

in the only way you knew, to be like you.
Forgive me for not becoming all you may have wanted,
since I had to learn the fatal fact of limitation and,

hardest gift of all, the simple joy of being. And having
uttered this, to cease wrestling with the angel and call him
good, then watch him, slowly fading, embrace the chastened son.

# Ghost

After so much time you'd think
you'd have it netted
in the mesh of language. But again
it reconfigures, slick as Proteus.

You're in the kitchen talking
with your ex-Navy brother, his two kids
snaking over his tattooed arms, as he goes on
& on about being out of work again.

For an hour now you've listened,
his face growing dimmer in the lamplight
as you keep glancing at your watch
until it's there again: the ghost rising

as it did that first time when you,
the oldest, left home to marry.
You're in the boat again, alone, and staring
at the six of them, your sisters

& your brothers, their faces bobbing
in the water, as their fingers grapple
for the gunwales. The ship is going down,
your mother with it. One oar's locked

and feathered, and one oar's lost,
there's a slop of gurry pooling
in the bottom, and your tiny boat
keeps drifting further from them.

Between each bitter wave you can count
their upturned faces—white roses
scattered on a mash of sea, eyes fixed
to see what you will do. And you?

You their old protector, you their guardian
and go-between? *Each man for himself,*
you remember thinking, their faces
growing dimmer with each oar stroke.

## Coda: Revising History

You know it's all bullshit
the poem you wrote about me
he said, over the golden oldie
on his tape deck, the butt
stuck between his teeth
as he shifted into overdrive.

You *think* you got me down
on paper but you don't.
It's you you got you solipsistic
bastard. And if you weren't
my dumbass brother and if
I didn't love you I'd slap
a suit so fast on you you
wouldn't know what hit you.
I might do it yet. How much
you got? I know you *think*
you got the classic tragic
stance of the *condition humaine*
but the truth was worse ...
and better. I know, man, I
was there a long time after you
were gone. For two days, two days
we nursed her in her bed,
her poor head rolling
with those sick accusing eyes
until I wanted her or me to die.
And sure Pop had a temper, had
a fist, but remember, numbnuts,
this: at least he didn't skip.
Try to get it straight for once
and see it from where I stand.
Words are whores. They can do *any-*
*thing*, depending on whose paying.
Drop the highfalutin mannerist
evasions, the this the that.

Keep it simple, stupid. History,
myth and God. Oh yeah? And who told
you? Look, one ounce of this
Hawaiian Gold will help you fly
a lot higher than that silly Mobil
horse of yours. Try to understand:
it's dead history, dead and over.
I'm tired, we're all tired.
Who gives a shit about it anyway?
You got your own kids now to think
about. For chrissake give
your head a rest. Dig it? Here.
*Here!* Take a toke of this.


## Then

Glint of mahogany, glint of those pulsing
neon lights, the far shadows in the barroom
buzzing, as he rehearsed the byzantine
stratagems by which he might address her,
afraid she too would fade like all the others....

Scalloped hair, blue eyes, blossoming white blouse,
this brightness, this Proserpine glimpsed
for the first time thirty years ago. The night sky
clear for once above the streets of Mineola, with
here and there a star. His Beta Sigma brothers, to whom
he had just sworn eternal solidarity, off
in the next room already growing dimmer....

She sits across the room from him, bifocals
intent upon her book, head bent as if weighted down,
this woman he has shared a life with.... Can he call her
back as she was then? Can he rewrite their tangled
history as he would have it, now the plot
draws nearer to its close? The mind, the aging mind,
which must one day see itself extinguished....

Expecting nothing, he found her there, there
in a pub, on the corner of Williston & Jericho,
in quotidian Mineola, in the midst of Gaudelli,
Ritchie, Walsh, and all the other hearts,
on a Friday night in mid-December, at the dull end
of the Eisenhower years, his third semester over....

How can such gifts be, he wonders, even
as he looks up from his book to catch sight
of the blossoms just outside his window:
great masses of late June blossoms, white
on white on white, flaring from the shagged catalpa
that seems dead half of every year, until against
the odds the very air around is turned to whiteness.

# Beginnings

They must have thought I was crazy,
getting you pregnant like that, one
month after we got married. I mean

not only the professors there at Colgate,
where I scarcely cleared fifty bucks
a week teaching four sections of Freshman

Comp while I finished up my Masters.
But the others, too, the more knowing
ones: Bill, with his Brooks Brothers

pinstriped suits and imported brandies,
or the woman whose high-strung Chihuahua
I used to chase up the street, till she caught me

barking at it and reported me, or the weedy
spinsters you taught grade school with.
Even, I suppose, our parents. Had the

scientific and sanctioned rhythm method
failed, due to some incalculable dissonance
in the harmonics of the natural law...

or was it just plain horniness? Things
of course turned from bad to worse.
I'd pace that ramshackle flat trying to make

the checks come right, while I read
Marlowe, Gibbon, Hardy, Frost,
and a thousand student papers, while you,

my eternal optimist, swelled slowly out,
terrified, and 300 miles from port, caught
in those six-month winters. I hope to God

my eyes did not accuse you for your giving
me yourself, but it was hell, those ten-foot
icicles creaking in the night. It was snowing

as we ground up the empty country road,
through those ice-jammed passes, to Oneida.
Forms, questions, the small-town nurses.

Thank God they baptized him before they took
the little guy away. Call it a beginning, this loss
of our first, this half-unwished-for,

longed-for son we never talk about.
It was then, driving back in the dark alone,
that I first began to understand the cost of loving.

# Quid Pro Quo

Just after my wife's miscarriage (her second
in four months), I was sitting in an empty
classroom exchanging notes with my friend,
a budding Joyce scholar with steel-rimmed
glasses, when, lapsed Irish Catholic that he was,
he surprised me by asking what I thought now
of God's ways toward man. It was spring,

such spring as came to the flint-backed Chenango
Valley thirty years ago, the full force of Siberia
behind each blast of wind. Once more my poor wife
was in the local four-room hospital, recovering.
The sun was going down, the room's pinewood panels
all but swallowing the gelid light, when, suddenly,
I surprised not only myself but my colleague
by raising my middle finger up to heaven, *quid
pro quo*, the hardly grand defiant gesture a variant
on Vanni Fucci's figs, shocking not only my friend
but in truth the gesture's perpetrator too. I was 24,
and, in spite of having pored over the *Confessions*
& that Catholic Tractate called the *Summa*, was sure
I'd seen enough of God's erstwhile ways toward man.

That summer, under a pulsing midnight sky
shimmering with Van Gogh stars, in a creaking,
cedar-scented cabin off Lake George, having lied
to the gentrified owner of the boys' camp
that indeed I knew wilderness & lakes and could,

if need be, lead a whole fleet of canoes down
the turbulent whitewater passages of the Fulton Chain

(I who had last been in a rowboat with my parents
at the age of six), my wife and I made love, trying
not to disturb whosoever's headboard & water glass
lay just beyond the paper-thin partition at our feet.
In the great black Adirondack stillness, as we lay
there on our sagging mattress, my wife & I gazed out
through the broken roof into a sky that seemed

somehow to look back down on us, and in that place,
that holy place, she must have conceived again,
for nine months later in a New York hospital she
brought forth a son, a little Buddha-bellied
rumplestiltskin runt of a man who burned
to face the sun, the fact of his being there
both terrifying & lifting me at once, this son,
this gift, whom I still look upon with joy & awe. Worst,
best, just last year, this same son, grown
to manhood now, knelt before a marble altar to vow
everything he had to the same God I had had my own
erstwhile dealings with. How does one bargain
with a God like this, who, *quid pro quo,* ups
the ante each time He answers one sign with another?

# Eurydice

A winter's tale. I was teaching up at Hunter,
a night class, nineteen sixty-six or seven.
Mostly stenographers and clerks, with nine-
to-five jobs somewhere in Manhattan
or the boroughs. Introduction to Poetry & Prose,
the *one oh one* variety.

                That evening it was
Thomas Hardy. *Hap, The Darkling Thrush,*
*The Convergence of the Twain*, the appointed
iceberg peeling the skin off the Titanic
like some sardine can. Bleak and heady stuff
for a bleak and heady time. Nam, napalm,
race riots, Agent Orange, the whole shebang.
And I was on that night, my best imitation
orphic voice, rhapsodizing on Blind Necessity
and Fate, the marriage of a massive ship—state
of the art—with some far more massive iceberg.
Hardy's Hope seemed a hollow thing in the face
of so much suffering, as I suppose he wanted it
to pale for the poem he was writing.

                No one to blame:
no grand design, no God or gods, no anything
but a rolling of blind dice. I preened myself.
After all, I was twenty-six, and understood
the mossy myths, dark and cold, that have told us

since before the Greeks how the world really works.
And then the time was up and the students
gathered their things and headed out.
I was packing my books and the papers
I would have to grade back in our small
apartment out in Flushing, where I lived
with my wife and two small sons, trying
to finish my degree against the odds.

                It was late,
past ten, and the wind blowing down the cold
corridors of New York. I meant to head straight
for the subway round the corner to begin
the long ride home on the IRT which, along
with other huddled masses, would take me there.
I looked up to see a woman standing by my desk,
Neither young nor old, one of my students,
as nameless as the rest. She seemed shaken
and her face was pale. *You're a good man,*
she was saying. *Tell me you don't believe*
*the things you said tonight. Tell me you believe*
*there is a God.*

                      Understand, this was *outré* and
unprofessional on her part, almost comic, except
she looked as if I'd robbed her. And for what
it matters, I did subscribe to something like a creed.
Or thought I did. But we were talking Poetry here,
and this was New York City, not some Podunkville.

I assured her my own beliefs had nothing
to do with it. These were Hardy's gifts to us,
the poems, written out of a world he had suffered.
True, he wasn't everyone's cup of tea—a brilliant
use of language, I warmed myself by thinking—
and the skeptic's view was something she might
sip on, a way of adding to the available stock
of reality we are heir to.

                    I turned towards the elevator
and bowed goodnight, then walked quickly down
the long cold corridors and past the guard out
on to Lexington, then down into the subway,
repeating Hardy's lines about how the *Immanent Will*
*that stirs and urges everything / Prepared a sinister mate /*
*For her*. The place was almost empty at that hour,
and I already at the turnstile when I saw her
following at a distance, her lips moving
with the cold.

                    I'm hard of hearing, and the train
was already entering the station, so I tried to read
her lips. *Please*, her eyes were saying above the racket
of the place, *you're a good man. Tell me you believe.*
Eurydice, I thought, drowning in a hell of her own
making, pallid and accusing, and I some unwitting
Orpheus. *For Christ's sake* (this to myself ... and then
to her) *I do believe. O.K? I do*. I do, even if just then
I felt nothing but annoyance, and to tell

the truth, a touch of icy terror. Please, go home,
it's late. Everything's O.K.

               A gesture only,
comforting someone who needed to be comforted.
She smiled weakly, a nervous smile, as if she'd
just avoided a collision with something
looming out there, immense and cold,
and backed upstairs to greet the vast and open
void as the doors closed after me.

               What in hell
had I just done? I thought, hanging from a strap,
the weary, deadened faces all about me.
What was this, some operatic scene by Gluck?
How badly had I just compromised myself,
I wondered, then turned to catch two amber lights
and a skull dangling from a strap across the aisle,
as the train went hurtling down the sullen rails,
lugging each of us to our final destination.

## The Republic

Midnight. For the past three hours
I've raked over Plato's *Republic*
with my students, all of them John
Jay cops, and now some of us

have come to Rooney's to unwind.
Boilermakers. Double shots and triples.
Fitzgerald's still in his undercover
clothes and giveaway white socks, and two
lieutenants—Seluzzi in the sharkskin suit
& D'Ambruzzo in the leather—have just
invited me up to their fancy (and illegal)
digs somewhere up in Harlem, when
this cop begins to tell his story:

how he and his partner trailed
this pusher for six weeks before
they trapped him in a burnt-out
tenement somewhere down in SoHo,
one coming at him up the stairwell,
the other up the fire escape
and through a busted window. But by
the time they've grabbed him
he's standing over an open window
and he's clean. The partner races down
into the courtyard and begins going
through the garbage until he finds
what it is he's after: a white bag
hanging from a junk mimosa like
the Christmas gift it is, and which now
he plants back on the suspect.
Cross-examined by a lawyer who does his best
to rattle them, he and his partner
stick by their story, and the charges stick.

Fitzgerald shrugs. Business as usual.
But the cop goes on. Better to let
the guy go free than under oath
to have to lie like that.
And suddenly you can hear the heavy
suck of air before Seluzzi, who
half an hour before was boasting
about being on the take, staggers
to his feet, outraged at what he's heard,
and insists on taking the bastard
downtown so he can book him.

Which naturally brings to an end
the discussion we've been having,
and soon each of us is heading
for an exit, embarrassed by the awkward
light the cop has thrown on things.
Which makes it clearer now to me why
the State would offer someone like Socrates
a shot of hemlock. And even clearer
why Socrates would want to drink it.

## The Dancing Master

Of all my dancing masters
the most difficult to follow
was Allen, for he could dance

a step so intricate, so convoluted,
my poor feet kept tripping one over
the other trying to keep up.

*Dante's line splits into Baudelaire's*
*preoccupation with the polis and*
*Mallarmé's narcissistic self-dismay.*

So he might begin, and I'd go tripping
foot over foot following first
the one step then the other,

spinning home from his class at Hunter
late at night on the swaying IRT
dizzy still with so much dancing.

If it wasn't Yeats's packed spondees,
it was the recondite word boundaries
framing Milton's epic, the hexameters

of Virgil transmuted into blank verse
clipped, or Hopkins fitting plainchant
to the chorus lines in Aeschylus,

then pushed to the limits of percussion.
Such dancing one learned step
by subtle step a dozen years ago.

Only this past summer, caught up
in one of his peripatetic dialogues
outside Assisi on the mountain road

that leads to Francesco's hermitage,
it struck me finally that, dance
as subtly as I might, I must always

stay a step behind, for his stride
was always greater, though I am
as tall as him...and younger.

Most masters were there, I thought,
to be overtaken in the long run,
or so Hegel has it. Though not this one.

One, two, heel and toe, always
another step, half-step, quarter,
with that intricate arabesque of his,

proving Zeno's math about the
tortoise and the hare. Fitting, I suppose,
that he should foot it first, foot following

foot outward, as we strode then toward
the grotto, me a half step still behind him,
both dancing toward the same silence.

# Steps

A cold wind rising on the creaking steps
    behind me: hard oak treads & risers varnished
        & revarnished these past hundred years,

built by some broken carpenter, ex-Union Army,
    in the employ of Alvah Clapp, who raised this house
        for his wife & daughters step by step

from the ashes of the fire that wiped out half
    the homes along this street. Ash long ago themselves.
        A hundred years, and again the chop-chop

quarter notes of children climbing to the reaches
    of the second floor, this time sons. The assured
        clump downstairs all but unassisted by their mother.

Prom strut, wheelabout, bounce and glide. The desultory
    half note pause, the scherzo footwork on the landing.
        Gone now: one to the distant province of Sonora,

my young Jesuit, learning how to bury the village dead
    in his less-than-steady Spanish. One intent on
        carving out the Great American Novel as he works

to keep his necessary half step ahead of forty lynx-eyed
    students. And the youngest, head bent beneath a bare
        lamp somewhere in the Bronx, Freud become his second

Moses. Gone now, step by step, and you know their mother
knows it: the heft & creaking weight, the rise
and sigh of each lovely ghost son's footfall.

## Early Autumn Song

Brilliance of the first fallen leaf...
pink green, yellow, orange flare.
Renoir, as you would have said.
Air turning crisp again, flushed

with the light of waning summer.
At the truck stop just south
of the George Washington on 17,
the sixty-year-old bleach-blonde waitress

cheerfully "recommended" the house
special, a goulash on which I gagged
in silence, while two teamsters yammered on
about the virtues of their outboard engines

as I drifted back to your death two months
before. Thirty miles south of here
they'd laid you out, your thin body back
from Chicago for your final homecoming.

Muffled talk on the wooden porch,
the casket sealed, the long drive
across the slag heaps and oil storage tanks
of Staten Island, then down Flatbush

in cortege past black and Puerto Rican
truckers to the old Irish neighborhood
and your final resting place at Holy Rood.
Among the sycamores and maples David stood

apart, arms about your two small sons
who stood like little soldiers uncomprehending.
And when the last of the last rites were done,
he touched your coffin gently—for which I shall

always love him—as we turned away
to our waiting cars. Five years of radium
and chemotherapy finished, the false ups
and downs, your street fighter's refusal

to accept the facts, the Mother Seton pin,
then the hard-won patience, the yellow eyes
and wig, the meal you made in March for me,
classic French and good, though you couldn't keep

a mouthful down yourself and had to half stumble
upstairs and to bed. David playing Mozart on the
baby grand in the watery light of that Chicago morning,
the shrouded elms arching, as your boys donned

their crisp uniforms for school. You stood
by the back door shivering, talking about
the garden you were planning for your new
home. Soon, you said, we'd all be back together,

here or home back east. Six weeks later
you were dead. I can still see us dining at the Pines
there on the mountaintop, the four of us.
To Chicago and your cure, we clinked our glasses.

To the splendid new life that lay before you.
In the still of that summer's eve, backs to the setting sun,
we watched our wine turn to gold before us, talking
of how we could have gone on like this forever.

# FOUR

# The Statue

A July evening, *venti anni fa*, the four of us:
Laura, Eileen, myself, moon-eyed New World pilgrims
on a Monday, in our Audi, with our delicious guide,
our Allen, up the steep mountain pass which leads

into Sulmona. Across from the Hotel Traffico
where we stayed that night, facing the Piazza
*Venti Settembre*, the only foreigners as far
as we could tell, loomed Ovid's bronzeblack statue.

Church bells rang their going on the evening air:
a semibasso eight followed by a flatter three.
The soft laughter of the strollers, arms about each
other, as it drifted on the hilltop currents.

All changed to air, thin air, except what Allen
taught me on that journey, not knowing he was teaching:
the exquisite patience of the man, this Englisher
of Homer, Virgil, Dante, & the moderns, straining hour

after hour for three baffled monoglots, so that
one might eat the bistecca of one's desire
rather than the tripe & ink squid one's language
had concocted. A kerchief dipped into the icy mountain

runnel & placed on Eileen's forehead, where we
had stopped beside the ruined farmhouse like the one
Horace speaks of in his letters, while I paced up
& down beside the car, clueless to her pain,

impatient for her color to return. The look
he flashed me then through those thick-rimmed glasses
which had seen so much, light blazing into darkness,
the way angels, he once told me, address each other.

As on the morning of our departure from Sulmona,
when I looked up from my coffee to catch him
standing there, his eyes already on his statue,
having crossed eighty generations to have it out

with that grand old polytheist, seachanging Ovid,
Sad-Seigneur-of-Scrutinists, his glittering,
red-rimmed eyes aglint once more, while Ovid's
shifting bronze-black surface glinted back.

## As Mirandola Had It, The Mirror of the Soul

The convict's crossed & deep-set eyes
as he tilts back his John Deere baseball cap
stare unblinking at me, insisting
on the inverted black Mass symbol of his poem:
how Jesus is nothing more than some bludgeoned bat,
one wing folded back behind him and the other splayed,
this bright exegete who gave the coup de grace
to four flamboyant "homos" in Atlanta.
Or the other one beside him with the shifting

doe-brown eyes: here because some honky
in some liquor store outside Augusta tried to pull
a Magnum on him & caught it clean between the eyes.
He holds me to this spot with nothing more
than his lulling baritone and flexed beseechments,
and, yes, his oblique & furtive glance.

Consider too the downcast eyes of the Baptist
minister as we drive back into Macon, as he goes on
about the hard time he's had of it to get a hearing
for his prisoners, as if, he hurts me with his deep
convictions, we were not all trapped within
the prison of the self. He ticks off the names
of those waiting for the chair at Jacksonville,
until I too walk the dim-lit smoking corridors
& catch the eyes of men who acted as I myself
well might have done out of hate or fear or passion.

I have beat my head against the bars too long
and the truth is I am tired. I need the steady gaze
to lead me inward, as Plato's pupil, Mirandola,
tells us, where the soul's eyes go deep enough
to behold the green-gold globes of Eden's
inward-spreading orchards, the turn from what
the furtive bathroom mirror reveals each night
to a river babbling to the laughing trees beyond, where
some truer self keeps singing to its poor lost shattered self.

# For the Union Dead at Andersonville

Buried minie balls, splintered bone,
empty wells & cisterns. Andersonville,
Georgia, on a late winter's afternoon:
the ghostly phalanx of the Union dead,
row on row, 13,000 weak, withering
with gangrene, dysentery, cold & diarrhea,
the bullet to the brain as they touched or stumbled
against the dead-line: a soup of maggots along
this sinkhole in the cricket-maddened heat.

Whitman at Annapolis the week before
the lilacs & the pistol bloom'd, watching
the first boatloads of Union boys returning
from this death camp, his words struggling
to capture what was there before him. "Worse,"
he said, "than any battlefield," these "little livid
brown, ashstreak'd monkey-looking dwarfs,
these mummied dwindled corpses lying there,
horror in their eyes, teeth showing through the lips."
This prototype of Auschwitz, where now
the grass rustles and cold clouds graze in this
Georgian scene just beyond the gas pumps. And this:
this spring of water, water marked "unfit for drinking,"
which now I force myself to drink, the same
that served as solace for so many sick and dying men,
as once another desert spring fed those at Meribah.

# On the Sublime

When Burke stared into the heart of the Sublime
his singed eyes bled at what he saw. Even
Longinus had it wrong. *Terror* is at
the heart of it, a sort of noble terror. By way

of metaphor he thought of a man's flesh
torn off and scattered bit by bit, a fitting
end to whoever would tear apart the State.
It was the ecstasy of suffering made Burke swoon:

the way the victim's teeth grit on edge, the hair
flares out, the forehead puckers like a prune,
the eyes roll inward. Then the voice becomes
an animal's, a staccato scale of shrieks and groans,

pain registered in nearly perfect fifths. He knew too
that terror has the same effect on us and that, so long
as we are not the ones dismembered, a delicious terror,
which is but another name for the Sublime.

When the Reign of Terror struck, Kant struck back
with yet another formulation. By way of metaphor
he chose the raging sea. When the storm drowns us,
he saw, it washes out our shouts. Waves rise and fall

and crash against the cliffs, and sheets of lightning
shake us to the very core. We feel dismembered, yes,
as if swallowed up in death, until the mind assumes
a demon power of its own and becomes the very storm.

Consider Turner's painting of the House of Lords
in flames. In disbelief the people stare like horses
trapped in burning stalls as the flames embrace them,
until the frizzled trees and scorching air themselves

become the flames on which they stare, so that
we who look upon the scene want to flee beyond
the frame, which cannot hold those all-consuming flames.
Gods that we would be, we have our own Sublime

and stare in an orgasmic trance of terror at the pillar
of cloud billowing upward before our dancing eyes.
Let there be light, we sigh. Let there be light brighter
than ten thousand suns.... And suddenly there is.

## On the Limits of Transcendence

After all these months the dancing
heel & toe has ended. Clear the ground
of gawkers, Romanenko snaps, weary
of all the going round and round and round.
William Carlos Williams, hammered

into silence by his five bold strokes,
found a way to dance, his great left
forefinger stuttering the keys,
and sing of how the first man
danced in space. It was spring,

and the young earth trilled
with flowers. He thought back
to the dead Mayakovsky,
whose lines had roared & lifted
like Homer's polyvalvèd sea

of a man's brief going forth
and coming home. Now Romanenko too
falls swiftly back to earth.
He grins broadly for the camera
and wolfs down pickles, cheese,

& coarse Russian bread, hoping
for his feet to spring back to him.
He knows now his bones were not made
for such prolonged *exstasis*.
In the long afternoons the old moon

walkers rust, & the first men
back from Mars, they say, may have to
hobble down the streets of Petrograd
or Cleveland, their leached limbs
chalked & brittle. For two months now

my own right arm, numb
& atrophying nicely, follows after,
trying not to whimper, each day
learning how to live on less & less.
The ear grows patient & listens

& the mouth sings whatever song
is there to offer up itself,
flight towards and flight from
being what the singer hears things saying.
A time for dancing and an end to dance.


## Landscape with Dog

Often up the back steps he came
bearing gifts: frozen squirrels,
sodden links of sausage, garter
snakes, the odd sneaker. The gnarled
marks are still there as witness that,
confined, he took his tensions out
on doors & tables. And life went on,
& mornings, peace & war, good times
& depressions. Pale sticks turned
to trees, boys to larger boys, then men.
Ice storms, wakes, elections came & went.
And always he was there, like air,
a good wife. But then there's this

to think about & think about again:
the last time I saw Sparky he was dying.
His legs trembled & he kept moping
after me. I remember trying to get
the stubborn mower started, June blazing
& grease & six-inch grass & sweat,
& no time then to stop to pet a dog.
And having no time left himself,
Sparky simply lifted off those
cog-wheel scrawny legs of his,
& turned, one of the best things      .
life ever handed me, and lay down
somewhere in the woods to die.


## A Bad Joke

Because they had to cut deep
to get the cancer in his throat,
my father-in-law was wheezing out

this joke in his old stage manner,
the one about the woman who tells
the butcher to keep on slicing

till he's halfway through
the roast beef before she tells him
*dat's good dankyou now I'll take*

*the next two pieces.* I took him
by the arm as we crossed the street,
one eye on the lookout for idiots

peeling up the avenue, the other
on those hip-cracking ice slicks
(the Christmas sun up over

the new high-rises useless
to stop the wind from moaning
off the ocean) and thinking

all the while of my fifteen-year-old
son, whose voice has begun to boom-
bellow into manhood now and who just

last week was joking at the kitchen
table when all at once I could see
his lanky frame start shaking

as the thing crawled crab-like over him
again: his fear of turning into elements
the way the kid in Chem class told him

happens when you die, so that I tried
to hold him had as he pushed past me,
telling him he didn't have to worry

while he had his old man there, for which
white lie, or worse, bad joke, I beg him
some day to forgive me.

# Catalpa

In the patch-bright shadow of the flowering catalpa,
limbs loam-streaked from struggling with the narrow
plank & cranky barrow I kept emptying into the maws
of cedar boxes Mark was building, and stunned too
with the heat & the black flies' stinging, I found myself
once more shouting, this time at John, my youngest,
over the all-important inconsequential, when Mark,
leaning on his ten-pound sledge,
decreed there'd be no fighting in his garden.

His quip caught me by surprise. No fighting
in the garden. Off limits to all squabbles.
Fair enough. I tossed the keys to John & told him
to be careful, then turned to work again with Mark,
who knew more than me about how to build a garden
& could use the old man for his gofer.

I was willing. After all, we both wanted
garden boxes for his mother: boxes spilling over
with all those flowers a city boy can taste & see
even if he doesn't have their names by heart:
sunburst day's eye, blue bachelor button,
foxglove, pansy, pinkpurple phlox, petunia,
gladioli, iris, closebudded copper mums and roses,
stippled lilies like the yellow-orange day & magenta tiger,
indian brush aflame with brilliant tongues of fire,
gentle lamb's ear & the giant blowfish spiny purple thistle,

as well as all those whose names I never knew
or have forgotten (though somewhere they are
written down & somewhere they exist).

Sure, it was all bare black soil now. Mere promise only.
On the gentle rolling slope old moss & thorny hedges,
then the clearing of the field with one tenth hope & nine tenths
back-break toil. But she'd wanted flowers & we would
give her flowers, in handfuls flowers, from her husband
& her sons as in the mind's deep eye one could see
they would make her smile & smile & smile yet again.

At least in time. But here was Adam with a touch
of tendonitis flaring in his elbow from the lifting,
& a son about his business in the unformed garden
dreaming flowers, dreaming green thoughts
in a graygreen place he might recover with his father.
He seemed to understand that if the old man
would only stand still long enough to listen
there might be flowers for his mother everywhere.

## Sarcophagus

Anger so hot, so thick & clotted,
it drowned out even expletives & grunts.
They wouldn't and they wouldn't
oh God they wouldn't

until the tide of blood had risen
to my eyes & I had damned them,
punishing the poor coughing Pinto
all the way to Greenfield to get the lime

myself & saw the two of them
as I shot back into the driveway (denting
the goddamn crankcase as I did)
cutting the lawn at last: that undulating

seagreen half an acre they said they couldn't
&, no, they wouldn't ever do. *Get out,*
I shouted, *get the hell out now,* as in Masaccio's
expulsion from the garden, so that they

dropped the rake & left the mower there
mid-swath as I began to lug
the bags of lime myself that squatted
in the trunk like lopped sharks' carcasses

& caught the bag against the metal latch,
lime exploding over hair & nose & eyes—
such cool, sweet, flesh-eating lime,
& put my head against the raised trunk lid,

a clown in white face, defeated by my anger,
so that my sons could see their father's nakedness
as they tread water out of there, too
scared to help, too smart at least to laugh.

Something in my battered dogbrain whimpered
to let go & die, until a great sargasso frigid
briny calm washed over me & I was slipping
through the makeshift ice hole into

the stunned silence of a bluegreen gray
of ribbed & mottled shapes. No gawky flatfoot
wobblers now, the massive emperor penguins
hurtled in balletic arabesque above my head

skimming the underbelly of the floe, indifferent
to my presence. I must have turned, then,
scissoring down into the purple depths
sequestered there to witness squid and horny mollusk,

translucent fetal shrimp, the blue & phosphorescent
spiderforms that palpitate at zero centigrade
plus two: here at the very edge of life itself
where Dante thought the Mount of Purgatory

rose, purple-blackened bands that signify
the depths and then the void.
Far above I caught the air hole icing over,
and saw the shadow figures who had been

my sons wait until the hole filled in,
then turn to other voices calling from the shore.
Alone at last, I stared into those depths to catch
the figure of my father standing at the county

airport gate alone this April, hands folded,
while the twin-engine Beechcraft labored up
& up above the purple wetlands against
the coming night as I waved belated recognition

though he could not see me. *Forgive me father*,
I heard something in me breaking, as now
the lime began to burn the sockets of my eyes.
*Forgive me for whatever grief I caused you.*

But the depths had grown beyond my telling,
where a face had waited all these many years
drifting in this frigid stillness. It was limewhite
& seemed at home here in the perfect zero cold.

# Salvage Operations

When my oldest boy calls home (collect)
via satellite, his small voice
sounds as if he were just around the corner
instead of halfway round the world.

He tells us, yes, he will have to have
the operation there in Taiwan: general
anesthetic & a week-long stay in semi-
private quarters, & keeps playing

the same facts over, unwilling
to hang up, while I watch my phone bill
yanked screaming into orbit.
I am all abrupt advice, while my wife,

on the phone inside, remains solicitude itself,
so that, hanging up, I know
I've screwed it up again, having learned
nothing of what it costs to play the father.

And so I will have to go back down
another time to see what I can see,
dredging up once more the ill-lit nightmare
which stars my father and myself.

Trapped behind the wheel again,
I will watch with horror the ancient
Plymouth sink into the black canal.
Once again I will try to kick the window out

while I wrestle for a mouth of air,
cold water rising to the roof, until
everything goes numb. And once the winch
has finally dragged me up, I watch

my father watching. He slides a hand
across the chilly hood, then lets it ride
the green teeth of the broken window.
He knows there's nothing left inside

for him to work with anymore. But once
the window's fixed and the upholstery dried
and cleaned, he figures he could still
get something for the Plymouth.

# The Eastern Point Meditations

*It was during this time that a serious disturbance broke out in connection with the Way. A silversmith called Demetrius, who employed a large number of craftsmen making silver shrines of Diana, called a meeting of his own men with others in the same trade. "As you men know," he said, "it is on this industry that we depend for our prosperity. Now you must have seen and heard how, not just in Ephesus but nearly everywhere in Asia, this man Paul has persuaded and converted a great number of people with his argument that gods made by hand are not gods at all. This threatens not only to discredit our trade, but also to reduce the sanctuary of the great goddess Diana to unimportance. It could end up by taking away all the prestige of a goddess venerated all over Asia, yes, and everywhere in the civilized world."*

Acts, 19:23-28.

*We are always willing to fancy ourselves within a little of happiness and when, with repeated efforts we cannot reach it, persuade ourselves that it is intercepted by an ill-paired mate since, if we could find any other obstacle, it would be our own fault that it was not removed.*

Dr. Johnson

### November 5th: Monday night

In shadow, in late light breaking only now
from beneath the piled clouds, a milk-spun moon
is lifting, full and pale, like some translucent
wafer, as I race east at last, straining to read

the unraveling map beside me. Sweep of rigs
and a chill drizzle, heading toward the Eastern Point
Retreat House, leaving behind the countless lives
I've left in shambles and the twenty years they took

to build, not knowing how little I have ever
really known myself. Again the siren call of globe
and buttock fleering in the headlights even as I enter
Gloucester, searching for the lighthouse. *If you want*

*the desert, go alone*, my oldest son had told me.
And now, past the shrouded houses and clamant foghorns,
and the rise and fall of harbor bells, as I try to piece together
a world I'd lifted high only to smash against the rocks.

**November 6th: Tuesday dawn. Election Day**
Last week three large ravens flew low across
my line of vision before they came to rest in the branches
of a broken sycamore while I kept fleeing west
like Jonah to get somewhere I thought I wanted.

I watched them as they stropped their beaks
against the bark, their blue-black glinted eyes
upon me. *We know you for our own*, they cawed,
*you, whose eyes we mean to pluck in our good time.*

And now, here they are again this morning, a hundred
miles east, scolding in the damp grey air as they strut
across the window of my room with the cock-
sure arrogance of Kurosawa's bandits. Sucker punched,

my face hits the canvas hard. The crowd is jeering
as I shake my head, trying to clear my cotton-heavy brain
while the strutting enemy stalks above me, grinning.  And
the dreaded dream returns: all day we have held them off,

the enemy, my wife and I, our children in the hold.
Then, suddenly, and without warning, I turn on her
and fire. Her stunned eyes close as she falls away.
Drunk with it, I hail what I have always feared the most.

*November 6th: Tuesday. 11:30 a.m.*
Deep calls to deep. Down the dark hall to Father Drury
in his modest room, under the low lamp waiting.
He listens, head down, says nothing till I've finished.
*Two women, Father. As a man, I know you'll understand.*

*Need to sort things out, "accommodate" both to a complex,*
*necessary situation.* He looks unimpressed and tired,
as if he'd heard it all before. He scratches something
on a slip of paper, a passage from Isaiah. *Sit still*

*long enough to read this in the silence of your room,* he says,
then waves me off. Matzoh, bitter bread, hard to chew,
and harder still to swallow: *"Your safety lay in Me,"* I read.
*"But you! You wanted none of it. And I: I will flee on horseback.'*

*Then flee. AND, I added, 'on wheels, swift wheels.' So be it.*
*flee! Your enemy is even swifter."* Oh Christ, let me have
a little summer with a girl, and not the bills, the frets,
the daily round of things. *"Go on, flee, till you know you*

*have become a blown-out beacon, a tattered thing*
*upon a stick. But know that I am waiting to lift you*
*& take pity. When you have tasted the dull & bitter bread*
*of what you've done, you will begin to understand."*

Paper white, wafer slip of paper, crumpled *nuntius*
trembling in my hand, how is it, bitter as you were,
that you begin to taste like that pan dolce I carried half way
round the world once so I might share it with my family?

**Wednesday. Late afternoon. At the Lighthouse**
Having bent my knees or paced my cell with its cot
and sink and silent crucifix, having prayed over
the meaning of Isaiah until my eyes were stinging,
I have walked down to the lighthouse at the Point.

Step by halting step, alone, or so it seems, I find myself
walking this narrow granite breakwater. The wind howls,
as if it meant to hurl me off the edge against the rocks
until my broken body should sink beneath these waves.

Land's end: granite blocks slimed with the green
yellow droppings of gulls, until at last I must drown
or turn around. I think of my dear Father Hopkins
on his last retreat in Ireland. He was in his forty-fifth

and final year, my age now, a good man who would
soon taste death. And how, he wondered, had he advanced
the side he had sworn himself to serve? *Come away to some lonely*
*place all by yourself and rest there for a while.* Mark's words…

and my son's. So this is where it ends, with those insane
restless waves below. This and nightfall coming on
and a broken body. Nothing for it, but to turn around
to catch the light of the lonely beacon breaking up the dark.

*November 8th: Thursday evening. Nightfall.*
Maranatha. *Sit still,* Fr. Drury said, *and wait for Him*
*to come in his own good time.* So, after the talks, after
pacing the confines of these walls, knowing a full moon
according to the calendar is soon to lift above the waves,

I have walked out to the skull-shaped outcrop
of Brace Rock, past the granite, kelp & seaweed, to make
the top. A line of clouds covers the eastern edge,
so that the moment I have waited for comes and goes.

The lights of the retreat house come on one by one.
*Go back,* the waves about me warn again. *Go back,*
*or be cut off from the others.* So I will have to wait until
the dark grows even darker before I can see the light.

*It is not some school of doctrine we are after,* Fr. Drury said,
*but the schooling of the heart. You will have to empty yourself*
*before you can begin to fill another.* In chapel, in darkness now,
one more shadow among a host of shadows praying,

a lone sanctuary lamp flickers, so that our shadows dance
along the wall. And suddenly I am happy. For the first time
in months I am at peace. To the east, the moon has risen
in all its fullness, like gold gathering against a velvet dark.

*November 9th: Friday afternoon. 3:00 p.m.*
With two white woolen blankets from the hallway chest
I make my way down to the water through the overrun
garden path which crisscrosses the former millionaire's estate,
tennis court clay still visible among the scrub-oak and pine.

At the sea's edge there's a light so thick I could cup it
in my hands. I can contain myself no longer, *Abba. Father*,
I catch myself singing, remembering the children
in the choir loft preparing for communion.

Words of the potter, they were singing, words of the clay.
The Inuit speak of the journey to the Land of the Dead,
It is, they know, long & cold & hard. Which is why they line
the feet of their dead with the short summer's precious grasses.

*November 10: Saturday. Night Watch. 3:00 a.m.*
And the dream of the longed-for going home returns.
The watching, the interminable watching & the waiting,
the way a wife must watch her unsteady alcoholic
husband as if nothing has transpired, when she knows

as you do that everything has changed. Shipwrecked
Ulysses waits green-eyed for the suitors. He is sullen,
out of shape, & must struggle with his bow as he aims it
at the interloper he is sure he sees.... What does a man do

who has left his sons? And will those sons still listen?
And yet how blessed he has felt with those phone calls
home these past few days, and his wife's talk of those
who want him home. It is a counting off of beads,

two decades told already, the ageless story of endless
problems & of consolations which will end only with
his death. Or so he hopes. But to be needed once again,
if only to fix the sink or help his sons with homework,

and if that then to be taken once more into confidence,
and in time once more into her arms. She, who would not listen
when they counseled her to leave. Her love, her Christ-like
love to journey on with you, for better or for worse.

*November 10th: Saturday morning. 7:30 a.m.*
Like a fading ember, which the ever-shifting wind
awakens to momentary brilliance: in this the poem,
the prayer and love are one. I see I am the drunk
the morning after who, glimpsing the broken headlight

and the splattered blood and hair still frozen to the grill,
wants nothing more than to forget, and so staggers back
to brace himself with another shot of whiskey, or a beer,
or at least a goddamned can of sterno. The logs crackle

in the dark oak fireplace on this the final morning.
*Maranatha.* Consume me, Lord, until my grate lies empty.
In a cold drizzle I have come down to the stippled pond,
to watch a blue heron feed among the shallows.

Like some angel, at last it lifts its blue-black wings,
rises until it leaves my field of vision, though not
before I have caught the vibrant ash and blues
and the rainbow haze it has harbored in its breast.

*November 10th: Noon. Departure.*
*Ah, the radiance of those blessèd faces,* Merton wrote
a week before his death. *The huge and subtle smiles*
*of the Buddhas in the monks' enclosure at Polonnaruwa:*
*As if gaiety were exploding from the very rocks themselves.*

Our Lady of Good Voyage, remember me in the shoals,
when the swaying eelgrass like soft hair hisses
once more sweetly, and the sick self lulls empty love songs
to itself. Once a child in the womb leapt for very joy,

and a naked king danced before Your Presence.
Lord, be with me in the coming storms. Here on this
outcrop  I have come this one last time to say hello,
even as the waves keep crashing on the rocks below.

So here it is: the moment where I end and then
begin again, returning now to the one who waits there
for me so I may see her as the rock she is. Soon I will stand
before her, sea-tossed Ulysses, hoping to come home at last.

*5 November 1984 — 2 February 1985*

# The Peaceable Kingdom

Once my wife brought home eighteen five-year-
olds. Her entire kindergarten class. Yes, eighteen,
though I have no proof that was the number,
other than that was what she told me had been

there. The kids themselves never stood still long
enough for me to make a count. En masse they came
up the back porch steps, another teacher and three
mothers bringing up the rear. The kids seemed tame

enough at first, but as they reached the porch
I could feel their little engines begin to shake
the joists and beams around me.
Eileen & the big ones went inside, to make

sure the chocolate milk & cookies
were all done. I was to hold the fort
alone for the next five minutes, talk
to them, introduce myself, hold court,

sort of maintain order, you understand?
For maybe three, four seconds the line
or lines kept order, an order tighter, friends,
than what you may be hearing here in mine,

and then (like that) the whole thing fell apart.
The baby falcons could not hear
the falconer, the great invisible clockwork
spring that held it all together

suddenly went *boing*! as first one then two
then all eighteen began rolling head
over heels somersaulting down the hill
behind the house. They demanded to be fed.

They grew fangs & talons. They went
bouncing off the walls. Their shouts increased.
Except as an old pear tree up which to climb
or something to get round, I had already ceased

even to exist, and I was screaming
for Eileen. In a moment she was there,
and the unhinged revolutionary mass
returned instantly to order, pair by pair by pair,

with hot chocolate & a cookie for each kid.
Friends, I saw her take that Lilliputian horde
& read them all a story. I saw them flock around her,
I saw them feeding on her every word.

# FIVE

## Giottoesque: Christmas 1985

Hunched by the back door this frozen morning,
the sun a spangle-brilliant sluggish herniated giant
lifting itself over the low hills to the southeast,
I wave to my wife as she turns the cold blue Escort up
the glare-ice cinder-speckled ruts on her way to teach
her 40 five-year-olds (this is Bake-day for the letter B)

& thank the Bon Dieu for the warmth and alabaster
light he has seen fit to pour my way in his good time,
in this, the 46th year of my uncertain pilgrimage,
still confusing him at times with this other light
that comes from outside & which makes the blameless birds
to sing & chitter even at the turning of the year,

where even now they congregate beneath the blue shadow
of our majestic & denuded late-June-blossoming catalpa:
the blue of jay & flick of yellow grosbeak & the Sienna-
mottled wooddove, all accented by the gift this year
of two pairs of spectral cardinals. The jays are tossing
millet, sunflower, & golden heart of peanut high heavenward

with abandon, and no stray tom as yet hiding in the lilac bush.
And somewhere, over all of us, Halley's comet has come
again, as in Giotto's Christmas scene where it serves
as the Star of David flaming over that other sleepy hill town.
And with the still-fresh memory of Margaret & Eileen in the kitchen
baking cookies to give away, I found myself so startled

by the beauty of the birds that I rushed downstairs to catch
those parti-colored wings Giotto painted for his choirs of angels
who sang hosannas to a baby nestling in a corncrib to keep him
from the cold. And for a moment—in spite of our collective
losses at the Gander base when all our youth in a phoenix
flame went up, in spite too of our poor, huddling in shacks

and vacant rooms, who will, yes, be fed this season,
thanks to all those decent folk whose deeds speak for
the recurrent miracle of this turning of the sun once more
upon us—the heart is lifted up just as You promised
it would be by your unexpected brilliance in the midst
of all this darkness, where it seems You bide & smile.

## The Gods Who Come Among in the Guise of Strangers

Late nights, with summer moths clinging
to the screens & the shadows of the old stars
flickering across the TV screen, suddenly,
there would be Charlie's inquisitorial head
peering in the window with its shock of white hair,
followed by the heart-stopping aftershock

of greeting. Just passing through, he'd say,
and—seeing as the light was on—
thought we might have ourselves a talk.

Did I ever have time enough for Charlie?
Usually not. The story of my life, I see,
of the fellow, as Chaucer says of someone,
who seems always busier than he really is.
Then, abruptly, & discourteously,
death put a stop to Charlie's visits.
Summer moths collect still at the windows.
Then leaves & winter ice. Then summer moths
again. Each year, old ghost, I seem
to miss you more and more, your youth spent
with Auden & the Big Ones, words—
theirs, yours—helping you survive
a brutal youth. Too late I see now
how you honored me like those hidden
gods of old who walk among us like
the dispossessed, and who, if you are
among the lucky ones, tap at your window
when you least expect to ask you for a cup
of water and a little of your time.

# Saying Goodbye

At a signal from the undertaker's
young assistant, we lift the stubborn
metal casket, and I—as oldest son
and most unwilling emissary—lead
my sons & brothers to the plush cover
of the new-dug grave.
                    So this is how
it ends. With a backhoe idling
behind a row of maples, its driver
impatient to be home for dinner.
And this: a green tent sighing high above a pit,
words about the Resurrection choking
the claustrophobic air.
                    And now
I catch my father standing off there
to the side, his second wife beside him,
eyes gazing at the crumpled distance.
Ever so gently, my right hand strokes
the bronze side of her casket, about where
her pillowed head would be,
and suddenly I am whispering to her.
"There, there, Momma," I am saying,
"it's all right now. Everything
is going to be just fine."

## Then Sings My Soul

Who can tell a man's real pain
when he learns the news at last
that he must die? Sure we all know
none of us is going anywhere
except in some pine-slab box or its fine
expensive equal. But don't we put it off
another day, and then another and another,
as I suppose we must to cope? And so
with Lenny, Leonardo Rodriquez, a man
in the old world mold, a Spaniard
of great dignity and fine humility,
telling us on this last retreat for men
that he had finally given up praying
because he didn't want to hear
what God might want to tell him now:
that he wanted Lenny, soon, in spite
of the hard facts that he had his kids,
his still beautiful wife, and an aged
mother to support. I can tell you now
It hit us hard, him telling us, because
for me as for the others he'd been
the model, had been a leader, raised
in the old faith of San Juan de la Cruz
and Santa Teresa de Avila, this toreador
waving the red flag at death itself,
horns lowered and hurling down on him.
This story has no ending because there is
still life and life means hope. But

on the third day, at the last Mass, we were
all sitting in one big circle like something
out of Dante—fifty laymen, a priest, a nun—
with Guido DiPietro playing his guitar
and singing an old hymn in that tenor voice
of his, all of us joining in at the refrain,
*Then sings my soul, my Savior God to thee,*
*How great thou art, how great thou art,*
and there I was on Lenny's left, listening
to him sing, his voice cracked with resignation,
*how great thou art,* until angry glad tears
began rolling down my face, surprising me....
Lord, listen to the sound of my voice.
Grant Lenny health and long life. Or,
if not that, whatever strength and peace
he needs. His family likewise, and
his friends. Grant me too the courage
to face death when it shall notice me,
when I shall still not understand why
there is so much sorrow in the world.
Teach me to stare down those lowered horns
on the dead-end street that shall have no alleys
and no open doors. And grant me the courage
*then* to still sing to thee, *how great thou art.*

# Pietà

New Year's Eve, a party at my brother's.
Hats, favors, the whole shebang, as we waited
for one world to die into another.

And still it took three martinis before
she could bring herself to say it. How
the body of her grown son lay alone there

in the ward, just skin & bone, the nurses
masked & huddled in the doorway, afraid
to cross over into a world no one seemed

to understand. This was a dozen years ago,
you have to understand, before the thing
her boy had became a household word.

Consider Martha. Consider Lazarus four days gone.
If only you'd been here, she says, if only
you'd been here. And no one now to comfort her,

no one except this priest, she says, an old
friend who'd stood beside them through the dark
night of it all, a bull-like man, skin black

as the black he wore, the only one who seemed
willing to walk across death's threshold into
that room. And now, she says, when the death

was over, to see him lift her son, light as a baby
with the changes death had wrought, and cradle him
like that, then sing him on his way, a cross

between a lullaby & blues, *mmm hmmm*, while
the nurses, still not understanding what they saw,
stayed outside and watched them from the door.


## The Great Wheel

In the Tuileries we came upon the Great Wheel
rising gargantuan above the trees. Evening
was coming on. An after-dinner stroll, descending
by easy stages toward the river, a bridge of leaves
above us, broken here and there by street lights
 coming on. Our time here nearly over, our return

home a shadow hovering. Paris, city of returns,
you said, for the pleasure of it, like the Great Wheel
looming there above us, all steel & light
& music, daredevil daunting, against the evening
sky with the tower in the distance winking. The leaves
still held firmly, the unthinkable descending

of what lay ahead undreamt of still, death descending
inevitably as the Great Wheel in its return,
 (a descent first through summer's golden leaves
and then bare ruined branches), the Great Wheel
turning & returning. As then, with the all but evening
over us, our wives laughing by the entrance lights,

we rose above the mansard roofs, the trees, the lights,
lifting in a vertiginous ascent before descending,
as we chattered on against the coming on of evening,
our seat creaking in the rising wind, anxious to return
now to earth's solidities. Instead, the Great Wheel
merely sighed and lifted, stopping at the top, leaving

each of us alone now with our thoughts. The leaves
below, green, gray-green, gray, the dollhouse roofs, lights
like diamonds winking, aloof & distant, the Great Wheel
playing us, two middle-aged men, each descending
toward the Wheel's one appointed end, the Great Return
to earth, as the books all have it, come our evening.

For all our feigned bravado, we could feel the evening
over us, even as we stared down upon the blur of leaves,
our wives, our distant children, on all we would return
to, the way shipwrecked sailors search for lights
along a distant shore, as we began the last descent,
leaving the tents and Garden with its Great Wheel

to return, my dear dead friend, to the winking lights
along the boulevard, leaves lifting & descending,
as now the evening air took mastery, it & the Great Wheel.

# The Cistern

In the limestone cistern
beneath St. Peter Gallicantu
in Jerusalem, my back against
the wall, try as I might,
I could not keep from weeping.
*I am a man gone down into the pit,*
we listened to Fr. Doyle reading,
*a man shorn of his strength,*
*one more among the dead,*
*among those You have forgotten.*

And did he call upon the psalms
to warm him in his need?
The night before he died
they dragged him here to try him.
What answers he could give
lay shattered on the pavement.
Later his quizzers grew tired
and impatient. Let others try him
in the morning. Enough for now
to knot a rope across his chest
and drop him into darkness.

Hanging by his wrists, *Eli,*
he would cry out, *Eli,* and again
they would misread him, thinking
he was calling on Elijah.

As each of us will be: alone,

friends scattered to the winds.
Except for one out in the courtyard
growing cold, poised now to deny him.
Darkness, the psalmist ended.
*The one companion left me.*

## Death & Transfiguration

Down the precipitous switchbacks at eighty
the pokerfaced Palestinian cabby aims his Mercedes
while the three of us, ersatz pilgrims, blank-eyed, lurch,
and the droll Franciscan goes on about the Art Deco Church

of the Transfiguration crowning the summit of the Mount.
Up there I'd touched the damp stones of the old Crusader fount,
paced the thick walls, imagined Muslims circling below
on horseback, muleback, then ascending for the final blow.

A decent pasta and a dry wine, thanks to the Fratelli who run
the hostel at the site, followed by an even drier lecture in the sun-
drenched court, then back down to the glinting taxis, ready
to return us now to the same old, feverish, unsteady

world half a mile below. I thought of the old masters, so
many of them who had tried to ignite this scene—Angelico,
di Buoninsegna, Bellini, Perugino, the Frenchman John of Berry,
the Preobrazheniye (Russian, Novgorod, sixteenth century)—

and thought at last of what Raphael had wrought. It was to be
his final work, commissioned for some French cathedral, his early
death at thirty-seven intervening. For those who only dream
of some vertiginous, longed-for transfiguration, he would seem

to hold out something magnanimous and large: the benzene brightness
of the Christ, eyes upraised in the atom flash of whiteness,
that body lifted up, cloud-suspended feet above the earth. There,
on either side, with the Tablets and the Book: Moses and Elijah.

Below, his fear-bedazzled friends: Peter, James and John. And though
paint is only paint, we can almost hear the Father's words again, so
caught up in the vision was the artist: *This is my beloved Son,
on whom my favor rests. Listen to him.* Meanwhile, someone

in the lower half of the picture is gesturing toward the transfigured
Christ. He is part of the curious and anxious crowd
that surrounds the epileptic youth, whose eyes, like Christ's, are wide,
but wide with seizure like some frenzied Sibyl's: the great divide

that separates him from the others, as if he understood the same strange
thing Raphael came to see as he composed this scene: that the deranged
youth has somehow come upon a mystery. Like us, he has been bound
round with fear, and only the One descending as he comes can sound

those depths of cosmic light and dark, in which the young man
writhes honeystuck in death, though he will—the gospel says—be raised again
to health and to his father, in this prologue to the resurrection.
That's it, then, it would seem: first the old fears descending, then dejection

and the dunning sameness in the daily going round and round of things.
Then a light like ten thousand suns that flames the brain and brings
another kind of death with it, and then—once more—the daily round
again. But changed now by what the blind beseeching eye has found.


## The Old Men Are Dying

After the three days' watch, after the flowers
are tossed into a heap, after the last mourner,
feeling the coming on of the autumn squall, turns
and leaves, the crew comes to seal the boxes, caulking them,

screwing the tops down tight, to make them seaworthy
for the last long voyage. The little boats tug
against their moorings until they pull free at last,
begin moving then towards the north, a north

more north than any the dead pilots have ever
sailed before. Two uncles gone in three short
months. How the four remaining brothers huddle closer
together now for warmth against the coming cold.

Twice my brother and myself had to make the trip
south from western Massachusetts to New York to pay
our last respects. And what was there to say? That
the old men were dying? first Victor, my father's

dead sister's husband. Short-order cook and journeyman
mechanic, his family from Milan. Bertazzo lopped
to Bert. Strokes broke him until he listed badly.
One more and I will not come back, he said, and meant it.

When that one hit him, he turned to face the wall,
turned north those last six weeks, until the dark snows
swept him up and he was gone, without a word, as he'd been
in life. Then John, the burly one, his whole life lived

on the same mean street. Mayor of Sixty-first
and first, the neighbors came to call him, as his
Little Italy turned to swinging singles' paradise
all around him. In the old photos I can see how strong

he must have been, so that I do not doubt the tales
my father told me of his brother and, for what
they're worth, I have passed on to my sons. How once
he pinned two men to a barroom table by their throats,

one with his huge left paw, one with his right. How
for years he lifted kegs of prohibition booze
and lugged ice boxes five flights down to the old Ford
van. How he once raised the back end of a Packard

while a buddy fixed a flat. It ate him slow, the cancer,
ate his stomach first, and then the rest. Leaving
his last room late, I walked down the five flights
of empty waking rooms, saw the unattended open coffins,

each with its still pilot waiting to set sail north.
And what was there to say? All sorts were there
to bid their last goodbyes: those who'd made their mark
and those who'd missed. With the great grandchildren

all family looks are lost. The blood gets too thinned out,
the young enter a world we never knew. Julia
and Giuseppe: left Compiano some ninety years ago.
Settled in New York with a million others like them.

Their first: run down outside their flat at sixteen
by a drunken icemen who jumped the curb and splattered him.
Siciliano, those from the north of Italy shrugged,
then turned away. For what was there to do? Once

my father sat on his sister s pineslab coffin, roped
to the flat back of the horse-drawn wagon as his family
began the long procession across the 59th Street bridge,
headed for Calvary. Too young then to understand,

he smiled into the camera. But now even he must feel
the cold. You see it when the four brothers gather
at family picnics, then turn, each one alone, to watch
the ducks drifting in the stagnant pond. They stare

at the water in the last light of Long Island summer
and, though they never talk of it, brace themselves
for the time when their little boats will be cut
loose and, dressed in their best navy blue two-piece suits,

their leathery browned hands folded stiffly
right over left with the polished black beads
between them, they begin to drift out through the once
familiar channels for the last trip north.


## Fear

He looked down at his desk to find it waiting
for him, something emanating from the face
there on the page, too often in the deepest reaches
of the night. Today it was the face itself
that seemed to stain the world around it.
The trees outside: wordless, bare, unlit.

A busy day inside. Work mounting up, small
kudos from an editor, a stubborn paragraph
reshaped to both their satisfactions, two essays read,
a letter sent, three bills paid, a student with a lame
excuse off the hook because of his largesse.
Of this and this we measure our success.

Or so he had believed. But now the gray face
of his friend was staring up at him. A friend just younger
than himself, who now would always stay that way.
A friend he liked to think of as living on some
mountain farm, like Horace, the acid wit half hid
by the Wild Bill mustache and the drooping lid.

For a time his friend had sung like no one else
and his friend had made him laugh.
And now his friend was dead.  And if the truth
be told, his friend had written so damned well
he'd come to fear him, each squeezed-off shot a hit,
neither short nor wide.  How had he done it?

Still, he counted him his friend, one who could quaff
age-old Falernian with Martial, Bird, and Mingus.
Once, seated at the opera, his friend had kissed
his fingers to the staccato flight of some stout soprano
basting slowly in her painted armor.  Each had shown
him how to wring a music he could call his own,

and in time the man had made himself that music.
And now, too soon, the man alas was gone.  The trees
stood naked in the ghosting air. The gray face seemed
to wink at him. So there it was: his friend become
at last a book. Somewhere a fat lady began with dread
to sweat a gorgeous aria.  His friend was dead.

## Voyager

Beyond the moon, beyond planet blue
and planet red, each day further
from the sun she floats out toward

the empty dark of X. Having done
what she was sent out years before
to do, she gave up sending even

the faintest signals back to earth,
to bend instead her shattered wings
across her breast for warmth. It is

late, he knows, and knows it will only
go on getting later. He shifts alone
in the late November light before

her grave, as so often he has done
these past five years, to try
and finish what he knows to be

unfinished business and must remain
that way: this one-way dialogue
between the self, and—in his mother's

absence—the mother in himself. Epilogue
to what one man might do to heal
the shaken ghost which must at last admit

just how many years ago she logged off

on her journey. So that now, as the darkness
drops about him like his mother's

discarded coat, old but useful,
he takes it to him, much as
she did, to ward against the cold.

## Silt

How it steals up on you, this mortality,
dropping its calling card, say, after the flight
back from your friend's wedding, six kinds of wine
on a stone veranda overlooking the starlit sea

while migrants labor in the fields beneath.
One morning you bend down to lace
your sneakers and find your leg stiff as a base-
ball bat. How many times you told yourself Death

wouldn't catch you unaware, the way, alas,
it did so many of your friends. That you'd hie
yourself off to the hospital at the first sign
of trouble. And then, when it should happen, as

it has, you go into denial once again, while your
poor leg whimpers for attention, until at last you get
the doctor, who finds a fourteen-inch blood clot
silting up your veins there on the sonar.

Mortality means the sticking thinners twice
each day into your stomach, until the skin screams
a preternatural black and blue. Mortality's
swallowing the stuff they use to hemorrhage mice.

It's botched blood tests for months on end.
Admit it, what's more boring than listening to
another's troubles, except thumbing through
postcards of others on vacation. Friendly Finland,

Warsaw in July. Mortality's my leg, her arm, your heart.
Besides, who gives a damn about the plight of others
except the saints and God? But isn't death the mother
of us all? Shouldn't death mean caring, the moving out

at last beyond the narrow self? But who has
time for that? Six wines on a stone veranda,
stars, a summer moon high over Santa Monica,
cigars from verboten old Havana, live jazz.

That's what one wants. That, and not some blood
clot clogging up one's veins. No poet will ever
touch again what Dante somehow touched there
at the *Paradiso*'s end. It was there he had St. Bernard

beseech his Lady to look upon him that she might
grant him light and understanding, which he might
share in turn with others. Lady, cast thine eyes,
I pray thee, down towards me. I cannot take much height,

though God knows I've tried. Six wines, two cigars,
a summer moon over the veranda, where I kept tilting
outwards, my veins absorbing even then the gravitas of silting
while Love was busy moving the sun and other stars.

# SIX

# Epitaph for the Journey

Miles Davis cradling his gleaming
trumpet, three black jazzmen slouched
like hipster guardian angels just
behind him. Searing coals those eyes,

as they stare out from the photo at you.
The jagged blue-black mosaic shards
of Justinian's eyes under the golden
dome of San Appollinare, unblinking there

these fifteen hundred years. Listen long
enough, and you will hear the arpeggios
those eyes attend to. Hart Crane, doomed
pilgrim that he was, surely must have heard

them. At least his songs report back
that he did, descending from the giant harp
he called the Bridge. Lorca heard it too,
his dear dark lady, moonbright pupils facing

that blind unblinking firing squad. Father
Hopkins refused our four-bar player piano
measures, listening hard instead for the strain
of plainchant groaning off the stones

of Delphi, an ancient music flaking down
the Dead Sea cells of Qumran monks, or Monte
Cassino's choir stalls, before it disappeared
into the vast insolid Void. Others too,

they say, have heard it in the timeless
vortices of time. And now, if they have
anything at all to tell me, it is this:
my time, like yours, friend, is drawing

to a close, my one ear dead since birth,
the other closing down that much more
each month. Most go about their business
day by day. They keep their heads down

or learn to simply wait. Here and there
someone points or gestures here or there.
Unheard melodies, Keats called them, eyes
ablaze, then dimming as his body fell apart.

Once my own eyes blazed, but that was then.
Too late, someone else is singing. Too late.
But the high flung bells—if anyone can or cares
to hear them—keep choiring in the haunted risen wind.

## Variations on a Theme

Miami sunlight, as in a painting
by the poet Donald Justice:
a V of three pelicans drifting south
past the condos and the royal palms,
aflame now with the green scent
of coconut & parrot. Out, out
toward the Atlantic's darker waters
the pelicans keep drifting...

What is it we keep thinking of?
Of the brilliance of some perfect noon
arrived now from its opaque distance?
Or of the doctor, half our age,
who will stare down into the shallows
of our eyes, then turn to mark
his chart, as the soul begins to slip now
through the fissure of the mouth?

It is what we often think about,
though we mask it any way we can,
to think instead of sunlight in Miami,
as in a painting by the poet Donald
Justice, which shows the key lime
cobalt brilliance of the surging
gulf, and in the background
three dots drifting slowly out to sea...

**The Blank Canvas James Franco Says He Saw**

Out of the essential poverty of the self,
out of the blank page, the blank canvas
upon which we stare for minutes, out of
the numbness, out of the terror the blank
inevitably gives rise to, out of the eerie silence
laced only with the far yip of the neighbor's dog
or the angry jay swiping sunflower seed
onto the patient ground that has waited there....
out of the void, out of the ether emptiness,
you begin with a line, a swirl, a splash of paint,
a bold brushstroke linking dot to dot to dot,
like grackles on a wire—note, note, and a half note—
a squiggle of white and the half white you place just so.

Again and again and again, as you have your whole life
now, you start with a line, a slant line, a syllable, a word,
as you face once more into the unblinking white
of the page, fever-empty as some vast Sahara there
before you, the screech & skritter of the mind balked,
befuddled, unwilling to settle into silence, that sister
of oblivion, until the scrambled words stumble forth
with...with something like release, relief, and your
disbelief for the moment gives way to something like
belief, before that too drifts off, its brief life spent, back into
the black hole from which the blank smoke rose. Again.

# Unsolicited

Poem after poem keeps tumbling in,
Most computer-spawned, and in different fonts,
Some typed on onionskin, the odd one
Scrawled in pencil, erased, redone. One wants

To respond, if not in kind, then—better—
Kindly, to each and every one: the earnest ones,
The ones accompanied with the proper letter
Like a doting mother, the witty ones (with puns),

The ten-page epic, the tanka & the haiku (lopped),
The yellowed odes to butterflies & sad elm trees,
The mythy sequence on awkward stilts that flopped,
The embalmed canary elegy, decked out with fleas.

Week after week, the poems get written, mailed
To, yes, yours truly, with such high hopes in each one
It hurts to stamp them failed & failed & failed
For the odd one among the rest that sings. Ain't we got fun.

# Words

Midwinter. A coalmining town
somewhere in Pennsylvania. A man
walks pensively an icy street
in darkness. Everything is dark,
except for the sheet of windblown
foolscap, which seems to move
the same way he is moving,
until at last he feels compelled
to stoop and pick it up.

How surprised he is to find
a poem there on the crumpled sheet,
words scribbled down in pencil,
slantwise, half of them misspelt,
but fierce words still, huddled
there before him against the cold
like so much coal blue mummy corn,
the germ inside waiting for this eye,
this ear, to grow inside the man.

The man can see the words have shaped
the awkward air of the occasion, and are
the soundings of some wounded soul,
a soul charred perhaps by too much drink,
though it might be any wound—fear,
loneliness, remorse—needing to be
embraced and taken in, which is what
the man, who warms his hands before
the broken words, now begins to do.

## The Things They Taught Me

Except on those green rosters long since
turned to yellow, or asleep somewhere
in the vaults of Whitmore, most
of their names are lost to me,
covered palimpsest-wise by others
who came after, each class growing
inward like rings about some
tree of knowledge which sends forth
its yearly shoots, though I still see
many of those vivid quizzing faces
by the peach-blush light of memory.
* * * * *


From that November afternoon at Colgate
all those years ago, as a young man
patting himself on the back for teaching
so crisply & deliciously on death
& dying in the work of Hemingway,
then hearing the news from the car radio
outside the great gray shale stone building
that the president had been shot,
I understood that there were lessons
to be learned, even on bucolic leaf-strewn
quadrangles, and that I was just then
being taught a hard one.
* * * * * *


Or on this campus back in the spring
of '70, having left New York for the provinces,

with a fresh degree, a wife & three small kids
in tow, I watched as a nightmare war
began spilling over into other countries.
Young men whom I had known
were going under in leech-thick paddies
somewhere, while a mad karma roiled
over those back home. Dazed prophets
stoned on LSD & armed with bullhorns
patrolled our administration buildings,
which hunkered down like toad
presidios. By the flare of some brave new
order I watched ghost trundles
begin rumbling across our campus.
No one over thirty could be trusted.
A girl of nineteen, flowers braiding
her waist-long hair, played a novice
campus cop. "Come on," she coaxed him.
"Give me your gun so no one will get hurt."
In the lotus-fevered milling dark
she offered him a ring of broken daisies.

\* \* \* \* \*

With teaching halted, there were
those who came Nicodemus-like by night
to see me. They didn't give a damn
about a grade, I was to understand, not
while this dirty little war was going on,
unless of course the grade could be
hitched up to a B or better. Insurance,

I was made to understand, in case
this Mother of all Revolutions fizzled.
* * * * *

That was the one side: to learn
they were only like the rest of us,
innocent, filled with delusions, less
than perfect. The other side of it
was what I tried to teach them:
a honeyed wisdom gathered drop
by patient drop. From bouncing
my own biases & gaucheries
off so many captive ears, I came in time
to see that each voice out there
could in a single brilliant instant
reveal yet another ray of the great
& fiery wheel the prophets sing of.
* * * * *

How often their words, reshaped
& polished, like our Hubbell scope,
could open on galaxies of thought
I never knew existed. In the give and take
of my time-lapse dance before the blackboard,
I think I came to taste the Spirit's gifts:
wisdom, insight, reverence, patience,
heart, the knowing when to speak & when
to hold your fire. Otherwise what you do
up there before the class becomes

mere peacock strut, the pseudo-dazzling
wit which fears all difference, or the small
self-interests of the tenured jackal.
\* \* \* \* \*

"If they hadn't paid me to come and teach,"
some poet said once, "I'd have gladly paid
to have the privilege." My sentiments
exactly. Though bread being what it is,
& rent, & books, and having pored now
over ten thousand thousand papers—towers
of ivory amidst ziggurats of babble—
I'm relieved to see it work the way it has:
the being paid for what one loves to do.
\* \* \* \* \*

"Still, you won't know until the best
of it is over what the real gifts were,"
another teacher told me, who'd seen
forty years of it in classrooms just
like these glare-lit waiting rooms
you find in registries & morgues.
He was right, for what really came
to matter, once I was smart enough to see,
was what my students taught me, though
I never told them, the story being that it was
I who had been sent to do the teaching.

# North/South

In the long run for both of us
it will be the willow darkening
in some northern twilight
as the dominant key of winter

reasserts itself. As even now
in late August outside this window
the small birds hesitate among
the branches before they arc

their bodies south for the three
days' flight above the amber waters.
Angel-winged, each turns, then locks
on its quintessential homing.

Or, to see it from your perspective:
flight  to a southernmost extreme.
Robert, for whom if not for you
do I feel this bond, your north

anchoring my still-vexed south?
Even these free-verse lines
arc in a double *pas de deux*
pan-foot, goat-foot rocking back

and forth, counter to that
granite bass of yours. Again
you grin that flinty grin of yours.
"You still walk a little crazy,

but no cop could say you didn't
walk the line. What *you* have
is a case of free form hurtling
after form. Count yourself among

the blessed who still have something
to go home to." Robert, who was it
warned us to work while there was
still ember light enough to work,

knowing the long night was coming on?
The night: when all hands must willy-
nilly rest, the last line edging into granite
or the upturn of the wind, the same

which flips the feathers of small birds
as they chatter in the branches.
They too must sense the great change
coming on and so begin again

while there is still time to test their wings,
half shaped by years of trial and half again
by luck, before they turn—as I know we both
hope someday to do—into the very air itself.

# Light

Strange how it strikes you, that special light.
An old light, really, if light is ever really old,
a light memory kindles here within this afternoon.
Or is it light itself that kindles memory,
flooding in so quietly you start up from your
reverie to follow where it leads? A light,

then, a peculiar and very special light. Let's say the light
brightening a special place: a Vermont mountain
light, lighting up an inn and cottages, with green shade
by way of contrast to the impasto-yellow fountain-
falling light of some late August. A light made
for this very special place alone, a late summer's light

which falls upon a green glass pitcher on this old oak
dresser, while the laughter of those precious ghosts runs on
across the fields, rippling outward until it too disappears.
Light on a pitcher in a chastened Shaker room, where I stand alone.
How is it that this image lingers on and on after all these years?
fifteen summers gone. Gone at a single stroke.

And those I loved gone with them. Sad-eyed Terrence gone
and Gardner gone and Nemerov. And Wild Bill gone
as well, gone across the river, to be ferried to another shore.
And so many others gone, whose names memory has forgotten,
some gentle gesture all that's left of all that went before,
like crystal shattered in some modest palace revolution.

Gone too—though still this side of Stygia—Phil. And Don,
who used to sketch out in the lower hay-mown field.
And Wyatt gone, with whom I walked those roads,
& Mark & David gone, & Bob, of course, who would not yield
to time or pressure or those petty, toxic, academic toads. . . .
Gone, gone away, all my lovely ones long gone.

And Linda gone, and Nancy. My pretty ones all gone,
long packed and gone away, their shades still hovering
on those old laugh-haunted porches like brilliant fireflies
on dark summer nights. Gone, gone now, all of it, evening covering
all but these memories, where now only a light alone abides,
gilding this dresser and the green-gold pitcher it has settled on.

## Elegy for William Carlos Williams on the Eve of His 125th Birthday

A chic Italian restaurant here on Rutherford's
Park Avenue. On the corner across the street:
your home, sold to strangers. All those bright
flowers you & Flossie tended in your back yard

gone. A piece of still-warm bread & a bottle of
Chianti I had to bring myself. It's a dry town still,
where the mythy gods of wine stay suspect, Bill.
A blue flame gutters my lonely table.  I ask

the waitress, Cora, Cora something, who's worked here
the past four years, if she's ever heard of you.
A poet. You know, one of those. Spent his whole life
here in this godforsaken Jersey suburb long before

the stadium came to nest in the purple cattailed
meadows. Coaxed three thousand kids into this new
world naked, making endless calls on these same
ramshackle four-square rooms, leaving poems

at every railroad crossing, as he netted isolate flecks
of images from the sick, majestic river that runs
through town, heading for the black Atlantic
to be lost. "A poet, huh?," she says, in that

distinctive twang my poor mother had in life.
"Right here in this ol' town. Well, I'll be damned."
As we all are, don't you know, with our broken
cries and words. Again the dark descends

as she leaves me to myself. Except for the bells,
you were never one for Catholic rituals, old friend,
but let me ring one in tonight. A crust of bread
here in my left hand and a glass of dago red

in my right, which now I lift to you,
listening as you taught me with the one good ear
I've left for the river's sad and distant music riffing
those jagged Jersey sounds you loved so well.

# Annunciation

Three birds sang from the shaded grove.
The lilies shook and nodded, the white stones shone.
Through every leaf the dazzle of blue light,
and clouds chevying eastward out to sea.
And now…now, the pregnant silence of your word.
*This* is the moment I have waited for all week
as I have prayed here pleading for your peace.
Once, among the stalls at Marrakech, one man
looped a freighted snake about my son's bare neck,
while another shook a basket in my startled eyes.
He was grinning as he circled me, while I
threw whatever money I had at them,
begging them to take the thing away. And now,
like that, so quietly, a sudden breeze comes up
to kiss me on my forehead, the way a mother will,
when she sighs goodnight, goodnight, and covers you,
her sandal's heel firmly on the writhing serpent's head.

## Our Lady of Peace, Turners Falls

*On the Occasion of Our Three Churches Enfolded into One*
*January 15, 2006*


From French Canada they came, and the Polish shires,
sharing the rails west from Fitchburg, along which the Irish
toiled. Tall trees by the thousands felled, then sent swirling
down the Long River & the Falls, year in, year out, and sterling
silver knives the Swiss & Germans forged on those old assembly lines.
And the paper mills along the cold canal, which time resigns
to memory now, amid the red brick buildings standing still
along the avenues and grid of streets, and up along the hill
above the river, and those granite walls along the railroad track.
St. Patrick's Day & the old French nuns and summer polkas…. Oh back,
Lord, bring back the sweet memories of the Faith that bound
us all together, each gold thread, woof and warp around
and through the fabric of our daily journeys here
in the very place we altogether shaped. With all our care,
we thought things would never change, though the river changes,
and yes, we change with it.
                              But isn't it the Spirit arranges
all things in the end? And so this space, named for a mother who keeps
within her deepest self a son, her gift to us, so that the heart leaps
at the promise of it all, at what remains at the very core of Who
it is we keep coming back to…in spite of everything we do.
Lady of Peace, remembering your own sweet mother & your Son,
come this day and renew us all again. Fiat. May His will be done.

# Nine One One

Once again the nightmare. The blue-black plume,
The billowing flame. All my life I've been afraid
Of tall buildings, and here was the tallest, down
Near Manhattan's prow. Firemen and police officers
Kept running *towards* the flames! People were falling
Or jumping. No one yet seemed to understand
What was happening. How will they put it out,
I kept wondering. Then the second tower.
Then the Pentagon. Then a fourth jet, down

Somewhere over Pennsylvania. Reality itself
Seemed to buckle with the buckling towers.
"Mourn for the city," a man who knew
His Apocalypse quoted me later that week.
The Scarlet City, he said. All over again. Gone.
Gone in an hour. But who deserved this? These
Were folks with families, folks with mortgages
To pay. You or me in the right place
At the wrong time. Plans put on hold. Forever.

Nurses waiting for patients who never appeared.
A priest saying Mass in the smoldering rubble.
The dead, the many dead, and the millions more
Wounded that morning. Mother of sorrows,
What can I say? Here in my room, I watch you
Watching your son, the one they will crucify
In their own good time, as they crucified him here
At Ground Zero. A mother grieves, while
Her little ones wonder where is their daddy.

And where *are* the lost who paid with their lives?
A mother grieves, and my eye follows hers down
To her child. Remember, he says at the omega point
Of the final Book, Remember this well. I am
The morning star rising once more above
My beloved city, as above the homes of my Afghans,
Above my whole bent, broken world. Have I not
Told you I will not leave you orphans? Not
One of you. Not one, not a single precious one.

# SEVEN

# Mother of Consolation

What you look hard at looks back hard at you.
As in this icon, where the child with the deer-
brown eyes gazes at something just beyond your view,
this child king who spreads blessing everywhere.

Blood of his mother's blood, bone of her bone.
Identical the mouth, the nose, the eyes.
You can see he is his mother's son, and hers alone,
in any way one's DNA supplies.

If too he is his Father's Son, how can you know
but by what burns behind the gaze, or in
the innocence of blessing? And even then there's no
way to know until you touch the mystery within.

And for that you will first have to understand
what it is you gaze at with the same dim eyes
Too long glutted on the sensual, the bland,
The million million flyspecked buzzing lies.

The scrim of sight, we learn, is dimmed with sick desire.
The Buddha knew this, and Blake, and Dante too.
How hard, O how very hard to re-ignite the fire,
The inner flame that lets us look upon these two,

these two whose gaze gives back peace again,
but only if we learn to turn the outward gaze into
the gaze within, the child's eyes remembering the When,
and the mother's doe-brown eyes turning to gaze at you.

# There Was a Boy Once

There was a boy once went out
To find the world. And the world,
It seems, found him in return.
From what his parents saw, nothing
Ever seemed to satisfy the boy.
And as he worked his way toward
Manhood, he tried on everything—
Knowledge, sports, a two-piece
Business suit and a Navy uniform.
He tried on causes, and rode a bike
From Boston west to Santa Barbara
In the high sirocco winds to feed the hungry.
Likewise he tried on languages:
Spanish and then Chinese, even Arabic
With a French accent, and read *The Economist*
And *The New York Times*, and in one long
Summer read all the classics from Gilgamesh
To "those awful Modernists." And Sci Fi too,
and Merton, and a history of the English
Language, and the Chinese classics, the Bible,
Cover to cover, and once—in Morocco—
The Qur'an too.
                    Somewhere in all of this,
He heard God's whisper. Perhaps when he
Was twelve, and asked his parents for Chinese
Lessons, the only Caucasian in the class. Perhaps
When—at his confirmation—he took the name Ignatius.

"Ignatius?," the bishop quipped. "There's trouble."
Still, how explain why he followed where he did?
The answer's plain. The answer's complex,
Subtle, contradictory, yet finally very plain.
After two years in Taiwan, he landed on the Chinese
Coast. Heading north—so the story goes—
And travelling third class with dogs and roosters
As he neared Beijing, he heard a Voice.
"Well, what are you waiting for?," it said,
And may even have said his name, though he
Surely knew to whom the Voice was talking.
The rest is history. The rest is joining the Company
Of Jesus in California. The rest is L.A.,
Fordham, Seattle, Mexico and Berkeley.
The rest is Hollywood and Chicago, and
Wherever else he's called. "I did a practice mass,"
He wrote just before his ordination after eleven years
Of study. "And I am happy to say I was as stiff
As the tin man and as adept with the Sacramentary
As with a Sanskrit grammar. I guess I need
A little more practice before I am unleashed
Upon the people of God." Once his father also heard
A voice (the family always was a little strange).
"Don't worry about your son," is what he heard.
"You and his mother have taken him this far.
The rest is between your son and me." And so peace
Settled on the anxious father. A strange world,
This world of Mystery, where things never
Seem to add up the way you think they should.

Where for every gift you give, the Lord
Increases that a hundred. The proof, they say,
Is in the breaking of one's self to feed the hungry.
And who among us has not been hungry,
Has not wished for the gnawing void
To be filled with light? A boy went out to
Meet the world, and the world met a man,
Who understood that for every no
There is a yes if only, like his Master,
He could say yes and yes and yes again.
And so he took a cup that he would
Come to share with others, and on the bottom
Wrote: "Ordained to serve." And thus it was
The boy I speak of finally found himself.

## The Cup

This chalice, made of burnished gold,
rests in its place of honor when not
in use, high on the old oak cupboard
in our modest dining room here in Montague.
It's a modest thing, the cup, with a small cross
in Chinese red, in the center of which there rests
a more modest diamond, which once adorned
the engagement ring which forty
years ago I placed on my wife's fourth

finger there among the unicorns
sequestered in the Cloisters, and which
look out to this day over the fabled Hudson
toward New Jersey. This was the same ring
her catty girlfriends used to say was oh
so cute and so adorable, and which seemed
to wince under a Long Island canapé light.
And to tell the truth, I'd be the first
to go along with them, though the ring
cost me twelve back-breaking weeks
hauling bales of hay and rank manure
down at Baumann's Day Camp in Merrick
the summer after college, when I was
armed then with a degree in English and
—except for her—nearly zero prospects
for the future. A week before I left home
to begin teaching in the inhospitable
Chenango Valley, we drove down to
Canal Street to a jeweler her father knew,
where I bought the biggest diamond
two hundred and forty bucks could buy.

Understand: I did what I could, and she,
for her part, always made it seem as if
it were enough, love filling the gap
twelve twenties could not supply. And here's
the thing: over the intervening years,
as I learned to make a living, and that
a good one, I used to joke about

the ring, though it strikes me as I tell this
she never did. Twelve months later
we got married, exchanging rings and vows,
which I surely tested through the years.
In time our three sons elbowed their way
into the world, our oldest entering
Loyola's Company to at last become
a priest. And as the time for ordination
loomed, amidst the awful scandals
that broke his heart and ours, she took
the little ring she had for so long treasured
to a jeweler's somewhere down in Brooklyn,
and had the baby diamond soldered
to the center of the cross there on the cup,
a sign of something good that held against the years,
where now, when the late summer sun
spreads like blood-red wine across our dining
room, it makes the little diamond shine,
until it says straight out whatever diamonds say
in that language only light and diamonds know.

# Passage

So I opened the little book she'd placed
there on the table and half shouted since
she didn't have her hearing aids plugged in,
reading aloud the passage she'd pointed to,
the one about prayer sometimes being all
you have to link you to your loved ones,
especially where death or distance come
between. She turned to her husband
of sixty years, still working over his bowl
of bran flakes. Did you hear that, Phil,
she said, to which my father-in-law,
half-startled, bobbed his head, yes, yes,
though probably he hadn't. Then she turned
to me, eyes burning with the bituminous
shine of a girl of twenty.
                        I have known
this woman now for forty years,
yet never once saw her search my face
like this, with the beseeching gaze of
a baby robin waiting to be fed. Besides,
she was fast approaching the threshold
now of some great mystery. She wanted
to be fed and I had fed her as
I could, with the words I witnessed
turn to bread before us on the table.

**Wasn't It Us You Were Seeking?**

"All the while jumbled memories flirt out on their own, interrupting
the search for what we want, pestering: "Wasn't it us you were seek-
ing?" My heart strenuously waves these things off...until the dim thing
sought arrives at last, fresh from the depths." St. Augustine. *Confessions*

The lawns and mansions of old memories,
pale sea roses, the ululation of the willow trees.
These the mind strains after, and not the bully's gloat,
the barn, the bayonet gleaming like a tease,
pressed against a small boy's neck. Just so.

"You wanted something other?" Something other.
Something lambent, like the memories of a mother.
The red eyes of the photo changed to brown,
the fret become a smile. Presto, another
mother altogether, the lady with a golden crown.

My sister, likewise spavined by life's events
(we are pilgrims here and have pitched our tents),
has written with the very best of wishes, and added
in a postscript only now: *It's been a tense*
*ten years refusing to mourn a mother ten years dead.*

"Wasn't it us you were seeking?" Clamant voices, out
of sorts with this submersion always into Memory and Doubt.
And now radar picks up human wreckage on the screen:
the Past, dredged up from the depths. And now a shout,
as it flops about the deck. Raw, barnacled, obscene.

Father lifted the host above his head & prayed:
A small white sun around which everything
seemed to coalesce, cohere & choir. But
as I raised my head, the thought
of some old insult likewise reared
its head, and in that instant the arctic
hatred flared, shutting out my world
& spring, along with, yes, my lovely wife & sons,
a no & no & yet another no, until I caught
myself refuse the proffered gift of Love.

At once the host diminished to a tiny *o*:
an empty cipher, like some solar disc
imploding on itself. Only my precious
hate remained, the self-salt taste
of some old wound rubbed raw again,
a jagged *O* at the center of my world.
Ah, so this is hell, or some lovely ether
foretaste of it, alone at ninety north,
with darkness everywhere, & ice & ice
& ice & more ice on the way, and this
sweet abyss between myself & You.

**P.S.**

Who said "Better the past as book,
the story sipped in small and smaller doses,
then left off mid-sentence by the night lamp,
the final page a decrescendo in italics"?
Nine out of ten seem resigned to have it so.
I see Señor X and Madame Y, three rows back,
nodding their assent. Friend Horace ditto.
The past revisited without the noise or smell.
The way it was. But bracketed, revamped,
lavendered, with a minim dose of pain.

Or this: life surging at the end like wires crossed?
Roses, after all these years, come round again as roses?
Dry straw green again, the shoots unfurling, damp.
The death knoll tolling backwards to the wedding bell.
Embers beneath the grate by the great wind tossed
high and higher, winnowed into virgin flame again.

## Casualty Report

The car coming on, then crossing the divide,
You at the wheel, distracted by our earlier fight.
Blood on the dash, blood on the steering wheel, your
Sweet face shattered in an instant, so that the slant light

Still, after fifteen years, reveals the seismographic scar
Across your upper lip. Harm done to others, harm
To myself. After all these years my words, however
Well they're meant, fail like the useless charm

They are. Too many nights you've felt me start
From dragon sleep, thrashing in the chill
Eddying of first dawn, my heart thumping
Against its cage of bone, replaying still

The car coming on, then crossing the divide.
How many times I've startled into night,
Amazed to find you sleeping there beside me,
Like a brave new world in the uncertain light

Off starboard, a gift of such proportions it still
Staggers me. Live long enough, and we all
Turn up on someone's list: the accident report
filed by the trooper at the scene, the hospital

Bed with its checklist, where this time it's me awake
All night, or you an obit in the morning paper. And there
You have it, the latest casualty noted over coffee,
Before I get up at last to rinse the silverware

In the kitchen sink, rewinding the morning's latest
Tragedy over in my mind, the way I've done so
Many times before, wondering whether to try and get
The words right this time, or simply let it go.

# Mantra for a Dark December Night

At the cross between the word & silence,
between this time and no time,
between what the word groans after & the no-word
answering to nothing that is everything, thy mercy.
Lord, have mercy, Lord Jesus, mercy.
Between the Utterer & the Uttering & the Word
Lord Jesus Christ, Son of God, have mercy
on this sinner, who dares not lift his eyes.
Sweet Jesus, Mother, Father, mercy.
Mercy on me the sinner, mercy.
You who know my heart better
than it knows itself, you, my heart,
sweet Jesus, mercy. Who came among us
and took on our flesh, our tears, our sweating selves,
O Lamb, sweet Lamb, have mercy.
You know I love you Lord, you know the cost,
sweet Jesus, Lord. Be with me, then,
and let my cry come on to thee here in this room,
this lonely office, this wring-wracked bed,
this road this car this cart, whatever
(and what does anything at all matter)
Creator, Lord of matter, Mater God, whom
I have glimpsed beside the candle on the darkened
altar when I least expected or deserved it.
Lord, sweet Lord, have mercy on me, a sinner.

# Wolf Moon

My father, two months shy now of his eighty-fifth,
Lies weighted down by two blown knees, edema,
Arthritis, loss of hearing, emphysema,
Reduced to wearing sweatpants underneath his shift

To keep some shred of dignity in a hospital
Four hundred miles south of where I live. Groan
After garbled groan spills into my telephone,
Mixed with clumps of undigested syllables.

Once again my bewildered wife has gone to stay
With her father, diagnosed with cancer of the lung,
And her mild mother who lully lully drifts among
The stars and then back to her rock-a-bye bed in Rockaway.

Wolf moon, wolf moon, prowling the evening sky
As you have these sixty Januaries past
Above abandoned rooms where I have passed
Sixty years and some, tell me once more why

What happens has to happen. Tell me, bitter moon, why
The old keep moving up the line, dazed with sluggish fear.
Proffer me some drugged truth I can bear,
As now they fall away and we limp up the line to die.

# Death of the Father

*My son, take care of your father when he is old,*
*Grieve him not as long as he lives.*
*Even if his mind fail, be considerate of him....*
> *The Book of Sirach*

Tide out, & the long hall empty & the silent room,
the crumpled form who was my father hooked up
to the oxygen, morphine-drowned, the crucifix
floating above his fevered bed, the labored
breathing growing shallower by the minute.

This is the hand, the right hand, mottled black
and blue now with a hundred intravenous needles,
the hand that held me as a child and fed me,
the grime-grained fist that also held the ballpeen hammer
and the massive wrench, and smashed my face

when I was young and bold, and that I sang of once
in lines of stunned, astonished, underwater rage & sorrow
with this, my own right hand, some twenty years ago.
Done—fiat—at the Sabbath table, my siblings
and my dear dead mother bobbing there as sea-wracked

witnesses in a grainy nightmare replayed a thousand times
since then, one from which I never have escaped. And now
my time alone here with my father nearly up. When he starts
from sleep it is only for a moment, and then to fix an eye
on the stranded figure of his oldest son floating there before him.

What we had time to say in the forty years between
the oceanic then and now we have either said or kept
ourselves from saying, or said only with our eyes to be read
as best they could. Day in, day out, month after month,
I tended to his needs, gave comfort, and—if the truth

be told—received it in return… and laughter too. Once—
relieved to see me when the nurses had circled round—
he grabbed my hand and kissed it. Fourteen months,
fourteen exhausting months of it: the wheelchair strolls
up and down these prison corridors, the spinach down

his bib, the stories misremembered. And now, on this
late August night, his last, a silent yellow light floating
from the nurses' station reflecting off the crossbar
above his head, the room is growing dark and darker, so that
I must grope now for his poor hand, the right one, the one

I wonder what the years between—had he had the money
& the mildness he so much wanted—might otherwise have held,
the years which then seemed endless, and hold it in my own,
helpless as he is, then kiss it, blessing him for all he did or meant
to do before the blessed darkness bears him away for good.

**How It All Worked Out**

*Come,* the Voices kept coaxing. *This way. Now. It's late.*
The crowd, upon inspection, seemed ready too. Shook
then that wide stadium with shouts. Dignitaries in black
began the long procession toward the ivory gate.

My shroud (a single piece of linen, with matching hood)
seemed outré and absolutely right for whatever
august event should now reveal itself. How clever,
I remember thinking then, that the voices out there should

be shouting in a tongue I both could & could not
understand. *Come,* they seemed to summon. *Is this
not what you spent your life preparing for? Wish*
then for this. But whether you choose or not,

*ready must you be. Must be.* I would have fled
then, you understand, as every blood cell cried
out for me to do. But all self-will had died.
Surely, I warmed myself, it will be better for me dead,

or what's a heaven for? An ill-lit passage led
up a dripping ramp. Flambeaux there were, & dried
blood smeared there & here along the walls. I tried
to keep my mind on the line & the thing that lay ahead.

What was waiting out there by the ivory gate? Were they
friend or foe shouting for us out there in the stands?
A milky light beckoned as the line moved up. Bands
blended in the unexpected uplift of a way-

ward breeze. *So here it finally is*, I remember
thinking. We were even with the entrance now, & I could hear
the wind howling down the passage with my one good ear.
Then total silence and a blinding light. As I remember.

# EIGHT

# Making Capital

*I cannot in conscience spend time on poetry, neither have I the inducements and inspirations that make others compose. Feeling, love in particular, is the great moving power and spring of verse and the only person I am in love with seldom, especially now, stirs my heart sensibly and when he does I cannot always 'make capital' of it, it would be a sacrilege to do so. Then again I have of myself made verse so laborious.*

Gerard Manley Hopkins to Robert Bridges, 15 February 1879

For six weeks I've tried lassoing the wind
and come up with nada, zero, zip. Oh I *know*
what moved me then, what sweet whisperings of the mind,
but could not make those protean shapes sit still, though

God knows I've tried. Sunday Mass. The eight.
My wife there next to me, thinking her own deep
thoughts. Congealed light on the pews, cold as Fate,
candles guttering, half the parishioners half asleep.

And the priest up at the pulpit, embellishing a story taken
from one of those Chicken Soup series for the soul.
I kept glancing left, then down, then right. Forsaken
the place, as if the Good News had dropped down some black hole,

paralyzed by what the papers were screaming now
of scandal, indifferent to whatever the poor priest had to say.
Then, all at once, up there at the altar, I caught a shadow
stirring, as if struggling up the hill under the heaving sway

of thornwood. Young Isaac, carrying kindling for a fire,
branches his shaken father had ordered him to fetch.
The figure trembled in the ether, then gave way to yet another,
whose wrists they'd roped to a wooden crossbeam (poor wretch),

as he too stumbled toward the distant rise. But what
had this to do with where I found myself? Everything,
you'd think. Or nothing. Depending on your view. True, the rot
of the beholder went deep, deep, but deeper went the blessing:

the thought that God had spared the first from death, but not
the other, who among the trees had begged his father not to drink
that cup. All that history in a blink, as the one went on to populate
a nation, while the other—nailed to the wood—rose  from the stink

of death, promising to lift us with him. I looked around
the church, knowing what I know of death: the death of mother,
father, friends, the death of promise, of vision run aground,
death of the self, of all we might have been, death of that ideal other,

the bitter end of all. Nada, zero, zip. . . Except for that loop in time, when
something gave: a blip of light across the mind's dark eye, if you
can call it that. But what? If not a good man going under? Then
struggling to lift himself again, bent on doing what he had to do.

# Hopkins in Ireland

Above the blue-bleak priest the bright-blue fisher hovers.
The priest notes the book upon the table, the lamp beside the book.
A towering Babel of papers still to grade, and that faraway look
as once more the mind begins to wander. Ah, to creep beneath the covers

of the belled bed beckoning across the room. He stops, recovers,
takes another sip of bitter tea, then winces as he takes another look
at the questions he has posed his students and the twists they took
to cover up their benighted sense of Latin. The fisher hovers

like a lit match closer to him. The windows have all been shut against
the damp black Dublin night. After all these years, his collar chokes
him still, in spite of which he wears it like some outmoded mark
of honor, remembering how his dear Ignatius must have sensed
the same landlocked frustrations. Again he lifts his pen. His strokes
lash out against the dragon din of error. The fisher incandesces in the dark.

**Shadow of the Father**

How shall I approach you, Joseph, you, the shadow
    of the Father? The stories vary. But who
        were you, really? Were you young? Old?

A widower, with children of your own, as the *Proto-*
    *evangelium* says? I have been to bloody Bethlehem
    and seen the orphaned children there.

A small town, where Palestinian gunmen roamed the Church
    of the Nativity, while Israeli snipers watched
        from the adjoining rooftops. It is a scene not all that

different from Herod's horsemen hunting down a baby,
    though you, dreamer that you were, had already heeded
        the midnight warning and fled with Mary and the baby,

And though they failed to find him, you found him, Joseph,
    and raised him, teaching him your trade, two day laborers
        who must often have queued up, looking for work.

How difficult it must have been, standing in, as every father
    must sometimes feel. But where else did your son find
        his courage and sense of outrage against injustice?

How did he become the man he was, if not for you? *'Didn't you know*
    *I had to be about my father's business?'* Thus the boy, at twelve,
        there in Jerusalem. Words which must have wounded

though they put the matter in its proper light. After that, you drop
from history. Saint of happy deaths, was yours a happy death?
Tradition says it was, logic seems to say it was,

with that good woman and that sweet son there by your side. For the past
two months my wife and her sister have been caring for their
father, who is dying of cancer. There is the hospital bed,

the potty, the rows of medicine to ease the growing pain. From time
to time he starts up from his recliner to count his daughters
and his aged Irish bride, thinking of a future he no longer

has. When she was little, my wife once told me, she prayed daily
in the church of St. Benedict to you that she might
have a daily missal. One day, a man in coveralls

came up to her and—without a word—gave her one with your name
on it. Oh, she said, her parents would never allow it.
*Put a penny in the poor box*, he smiled,

then turned, and disappeared forever. *Who was he?* I asked.
*You know as well as I do who he was*, was all she'd say.
Joseph, be with her now, and with her father, as he faces

the great mystery, as we all must at the end, alone. You seem
like so many other fathers, who have watched over
their families, not knowing what the right words were,

but willing to be there for them, up to the very end. Be with them now,
as you have been for countless others. Give them strength.
And come, if need be, in a dream, as the angel came to you,

and came to that other Joseph in Egypt so many years before. Be there
as once you were in Bethlehem and Nazareth and Queens.
You, good man, dreamer, the shadow of the Father.

## The Fathers

From house to house he treks, and inn to inn, the feral dogs
following the exhausted donkey. His wife, tired as she is,
does not complain. She knows he is doing all he can,
but there is no room, no room, no room. In time to come,
that common *cri de coeur*: no room. He hears the clink
of tankards, the bawdy laughter in the inner courtyard,
the dogs closing in. It is dark, dark, but somehow
filled with light, a dark light which is always there, he sees,
though there are precious few who dream enough to see it.

My little grandson gets up from talking to his train set
and looks at me. Then, without the faintest warning,
charges into my arms, believing without sufficient reason
that I will somehow be ready to catch and lift him
high above himself as his shadow falls across me.

He laughs, knowing he is somehow safe, though
my left arm hurts from sanding floors and lifting wood
in his father's house, and the arthritis I have always
dreaded  shoots once more across my right hand and wrist
to remind me once again how time keeps running out....
At last he finds someone who will let him use his stable,
a cave in the cold rocks, ripe with the dank smell of donkey
dung and hay. He covers his young wife with the tatters
of his cloak, stung again by what it means to be without,
here where someone with his blood was anointed king
a thousand years before, before the deportations, before
the shod boots of troops speaking in barbaric tongues.

And now the quickening contractions. Joseph the dreamer,
Joseph the shadow of the Father, the stand-in, here in this
backwater with the name God's House. And only after
so much time has passed even Herod's scribes will scratch
their heads, trying to remember where this quasi-mythical
Messiah will be born. Something reaches down and begins
again here on this threshing floor, like those waters from
the temple flowing east, a trickle only of light at first, and then
the baby's cry, as now the mother wraps him in her arms.
And the man, warmed by what he has been witness to,
swears he will do everything he can to cover both of them
in his failing, trembling arms, knowing it is that other Father
who keeps him grounded in the presence of so much arcing light.

**What the Father Came to See**

How old the story is, we have come to see, and yet how true.
The kid's back home at last, knowing he's lost everything
the old man gave him, spent on booze and one-night
stands, a sucker for every sob story his friends had found
to separate him from what they saw as their inheritance.
And, now, when the cash was gone, and the kid out on his own,

alone, reduced to doling out ripe slops to pigs, while his own
gut growled for what the swine had trampled on, true
to their indifferent boorish nature (the inheritance
all such pigs are born to), the kid kept thinking how everything
he'd ever needed the old man had always given him. And so he found
himself heading home at last, even as his sick soul's dark night—

replete with hissing fevers—loomed ever larger. So, with one eye open night
after chilly night in some piss-soaked alleyway he longed to call his own
as he watched for snarling dogs and whistling perverts, he somehow found
himself at last back home, where his father—and this is true, true,
so help me God—ran out in ragged slippers to hold his lost son up, everything
forgiven, as the kid slumped earthward, believing his inheritance

had gone up in acrid smoke. But the father knew his real inheritance—
the only thing that mattered—was what the cold, indifferent night
had unwillingly given up: his boy kneeling there before him, the one thing
worth living for: his kid back home again, alive, his own
beloved son, chastened, yes, but somehow still alive. True,
the boy looked awful and he stank of shit, but the old man found

his deepest prayers were answered, that the one he'd lost was found
and home again. Time to celebrate, then, time to make a new inheritance
for his son—now sobered—something the kid would try to earn. True,
all of this would only come with the daily round of things. But that night
the old man meant to throw a party for everyone, serve up his own
best fattened calf, along with wine and cakes and song, oh, everything!

But then there was the other son, the good one, who'd done everything
the old man had ever asked of him, dutifully, and had even found
some satisfaction in doing it, if not much fun, and just then did not feel like own-
ing that he knew this ragged wretch who no doubt meant to eat up his inheritance.
You see him there, bigger than the kneeling son, truculent, the bleak night
shadows etched there on his face, and justified, if what we know about ourselves is true.

And the older son is right, it's true, which the father knows as he knows day from night.
God knows the good son deserves the inheritance which for him means everything,
But these are his sons, his very own, of whom one at least was lost and has been found.

# The Stone Not Cut by Hand

*The stone that the builders rejected has become the cornerstone.*

Nebuchadnezzar stared while the prophet blazed.
*A stone not cut*, stormed Daniel, *by any human hand*,
however self-assured or self-deluded. *Understand:*
*It is the Lord has quarried here.* The king's eyes glazed,

because all he knew was earthly power: kings who razed
entire cities—dogs, women, babies, mules, the very land.
Kings whose subjects, high & low, did their each command.
*A stone not quarried by any hand but God's.* Amazed,

the king fell back before the prophet's words. A stone
that would smash each self-important, self-made idol,
whether built of gold or steel or any other thing their throne
was made of. Yes, whatever insane, grand mal, suicidal
impulse kings could conjure up. *A stone shaped by God alone.*
Womb-warm, lamb-gentle, world-wielding, tidal.

# They Shall Beat Their Swords...

With my father's Army ballpeen hammer I'd found
down in the cellar, I kept banging on the swordblade,
trying to turn it back into a plowshare like the ones
the prophets sang of. Plowshares? Hell, what did I know
of plowshares? Once more trouble was stewing—

you could taste it—what with old Shermans phosphoring
into ash across the desert, and all those blackened corpses
on the road to Tripoli and Hell. My right forefinger
stood poised on the passage from Isaiah, searching for
the recipe for peace. Too late, the pundits wagged. Too late!

Too late for anything like peace. A thousand generations
since Cain clubbed his brother in some field, and a million
cries for peace, for plowshares, say, and what's to show?
The bells keep tolling in their broken towers for the dead
at Megiddo or at Manhattan's smoking prow, as at Shiloh,

Passchendaele, the Bulge...and now in some hell hole called
Abbottabad. Four Blackhawks in and one already down.
And the ballpeen hammer bangs once more as some blinded
prophet scrambles from his bed. Ah, my father, look how
the plowshares keep turning into bullets, and the bullets into brains.

## Fish Ladder, Damariscotta

Huge schools of them, home from the Atlantic: flakes
of iced mercurial steel, each body surging upstream
through the flint-flecked crevices as in a dream,
entering the crush of falls to reach the upper lakes.

Spent now by the journey, they have returned in a bright
kenotic ecstasy to spawn at last and die.
A salt-stung moiling everywhere, as each frenzied eye
diamonds the irised spindrift waters to fight

the killing currents and reach their final reckoning.
This is the way with those who sing the glitter
going of the final cry, the light looming in the bitter
coalescence up ahead, as if beckoning.

I too would follow if I could, but the body's cold
from battling nightly with the tides. Bliss—bliss—
they sang, though I was likewise warned that this
would mean the final wringing of the ladder's rung, the old

truth the shad and salmon sense: that we are bound
for home, whatever home means, waiting for us out there,
wherever *there* is: blue-black water or blue of air,
bright Abba or bleak abyss, the thing that will be found.

Call it what you will: you, the stranger who follows after, faring
forth to meet the Other. Call it the awful leap into the whirling
world of which we know so little, as self goes hurling
toward the light waiting just beyond the final, fated daring.

## Putting Out into the Deep from Gloucester

The sea wind whispers and the tall oaks shake,
their leaves shimmering in the August noon.
And now the dry grass wrinkles and the floorboards flame.
Saffron motes, a distant bird cry, this brackish sea.

What was it you figured the wind might say?
The oaks sway gently this way and that.
Like young girls they sway, their long locks
shaking in the golden green. They are singing

to themselves, something only they can understand,
the sequins of their shadows shimmering with song.
Like some burning bush touched only by the wind they shine.
For the past two days you've waited by the threshold,

tide out, tide in, then out and in again, as if calling someone.
Your old stone boat sits there on the shore, ready to take on
those deeper waters, as if it really could. Again
the plum-purple waves are beachward washing,

each cold comber composed of spume and granite.
And still nothing seems to happen the way you configured
to yourself, though somewhere out there in those depths
continents collide, and somewhere dying stars implode.

The frequencies of air are filled with foreign gargle
and all the indices are down or going under. "Nowhere
in Aquinas will you find a rationale for so-called private
property," father is exhorting, as his little congregation,

composed mostly of seasoned religious women, nod their heads.
Cold comfort there, you think, considering what you've already lost,
but the Gospel seems to back them. It's the scene where Peter
goes out into the depths to fish as the Lord has told him to,

and—behold!—the first fish he catches has money where its mouth is,
enough to pay the noisome temple tax not once, but twice,
for his Master *and* himself. Found money, no? Mayhap there is
a lesson there for you? And if there is, pray tell me what it is.

When Jesus, striding the blue-black waves there in the pre-dawn
dark, called out to Peter to come to him, impetuous Peter leapt
overboard at once. Somehow, the yawing waves half-steadied him,
and with baby steps, or like a drunk man on the dizzying

ice, began walking on the waters towards the bedazzling figure,
who stood there like some blown beacon beckoning him.
At which point, Peter must have told himself that this was easy,
so who needed him? Which is when the Rock went under,

spluttering in that insane gasping sea. Only Christ's fast grip
upon his wrist had saved him then. How often he must have
thought back on that shock moment to try and sort out what
had happened. So take a moment now, oh scholar of one candle,

and look up from your desk. The oaks are quiet now, and the sun,
that King of Glory, has since moved on. The clouds, like full-fed
crowds, are gone, and the choiring girls have turned again to trees.
They know that somewhere, now as then, the wind keeps whispering still.

## High Tea with Miss Julianna

*"Begin at the beginning," the King said gravely, "and go
on till youcome to the end: then stop."*

In the land of the JubJub together they had tea.
High tea, one has to understand, six cups of imaginary
tea, the good Miss Julianna Frances, aged two
and a half, and her grandfather, sixty-four. "How do
you do this afternoon, Miss Julianna," he began,
good manners there in JubJub Land
being understood and *de rigueur* between
the Professor and his finical little Queen.
Sporting diapers beneath her summer dress,
she poured her airy tea in cups with such finesse
they might've been in Queen Victoria's drawing room
instead of in his modest parlor. "Might I presume
upon you, my lady dear, for yet another piece of cake?"
"Oh, sure," she too demurely said. "But let me bake
it first. It will only take one minute." I.e., one minute
in her understanding, for they had time within it
for another cup or two or four or six or three

of Miss Julianna's very best imaginary tea,
and time for her to sit upon his lap so he might read her
all about the Midnight Land of JubJub and then confer
together about the best way to pick the naughty dirts
from between their toes, or which of her many skirts
her dolly, coincidentally named for Daddy John,
should wear, and which chair he should sit upon
if Daddy John were to be invited to partake
of tea with them, together with a second piece of cake,
which was humming along just fine in the imaginary
oven in the slowly darkening room. High tea
on a Sunday afternoon at summer's end,
sweet credences of summer. How better to spend
an hour, a day, a year? And Alice leading down
the rabbit hole, and him following into JubJub town,
and all cares left behind now, as the little girl—who would
not be little long—beckoned towards the still-enchanted wood.

# The Gift

*"Stay, thou art so fair...."*

This morning the sun came up
over the hills to the east
in emblazoned golds and whites.
Everything was shagged with ice:
the maples, firs, the beckoning
rhododendrons, the old familiar porch.
The world was a multi-faceted diamond
of which you were the center.
*Come*, you beckoned from the doorway,
*look at this while we still have it.*
I was sitting at the table, my head
between my hands, and rose
to stand beside you to see what
you had seen, and then—like that—
I felt myself lifted beyond
all my chittering cares.
A moment in eternity
and the two of us inside it.
And now, as I think back on it
it was enough, *pace* Faust with all
his bargaining for this and that and this.
A view from inside a diamond.
Yes, all I ever needed, I kept thinking,
standing there beside you.
And all I'll ever want.

**When We Walked Together**

*For Eileen*

When we walked together
in the cool of the evening,
walked together, you and I,
in the cool of the evening,
after the heat of the day,
after the long hours under the sweating sun,
after the buzzing words like black flies
had at long last ceased their querulous stinging,
after the questions, after the answers
that refused at last to answer anything at all,
in the cool of the evening, when we walked
in the garden, you and I, in the cool of the evening.
When it was no longer important
for either of us to speak, since the words,
whatever words they might have been,
would have been beside the point,
would have said nothing our hearts
did not already know, where simply being there,
there in the cool of the evening
was all that finally mattered,
with the long night coming on, and the last trill
of birdsong fading off in the distance
by the ridge of the tree line,
when we walked together there in the garden,
in the cool of the evening, you and I.

# Notes

## Mairzy Doats

*Mairzy Doats*: A nonsense tune composed in 1943 by Milton Drake. It hit the number one spot in March 1944. Popular both in the States and with servicemen abroad, some of whom used its nonsensical lyrics as passwords. It is the version sung by the Andrew Sisters which I remember.

*Andrews Sisters*: The "Sweethearts of the Armed Forces Radio Service," a very popular singing group of the swing and boogie-woogie eras, consisting of three sisters: contralto LaVerne (1911–1967), soprano Maxene (1916–1995), and mezzo-soprano Patty (b. 1918). For their volunteer service during World War II, they entertained the Allied forces extensively in America, Africa and Italy.

*Sesanta anni fa*: Italian: "sixty years ago."

## The Lost Father

*Herodotus and the Phoenix*: The Egyptians "have also another sacred bird called the phoenix which I myself have never seen, except in pictures. Indeed it is a great rarity, even in Egypt, only coming there (according to the accounts of the people of Heliopolis) once in five hundred years, when the old phoenix dies....They tell a story of what this bird does, which does not seem to me to be credible: that he comes all the way from Arabia, and brings the parent bird, all plastered over with myrrh, to the temple of the Sun, and there buries the body." Herodotus, father of modern history 5th Century BCE.

*Pancho Villa*: My Polish-American grandfather, Harry Szymborski, together with his horse, Red, and 4800 troops, was with Black Jack Pershing's cavalry troops when they crossed the border from Texas into Mexico on March 15th, 1916 in pursuit of Pancho Villa for his attack on the town of Columbus, New Mexico six days earlier. The expedition continued until February 1917, when the shadow of the Great War loomed closer to home.

**Christmas Eve 1945**

Dumont: In my five-year-old memory this is probably a 1939 nine-inch console encased in a  mahogany wood cabinet, which Charlie no doubt bought second-hand at the end of the war for his flat on 53rd Street. In any event the entire tenement, with the flat and television, are long gone.

**Fathers and Sons**

For some reason, my sister (age two), my brother (four), and myself (six) were sent away to an orphanage somewhere in Queens or the Bronx for several weeks in November 1946. None of us ever knew why, and the subject was never broached.  My best guess is that my mother gave birth to a stillborn sister whom they named Cecelia. But then that subject was never brought up either. My father had promised to visit us for Thanksgiving, but never showed, though I waited by my bed all day so as not to miss him if he should come. I can still remember the smell of turnips and turkey gravy as I was led down to the dinghy dining hall for Thanksgiving dinner.

**Show & Tell**

*Bart Giamatti*: Angelo Bartlett "Bart" Giamatti (1938–1989). President of Yale University and later Commissioner of Major League Baseball. A scholar of the Italian Renaissance, he once wrote that "All play aspires to the condition of paradise." With play, "we hope to achieve a state that our larger Greco-Roman, Judeo-Christian culture has always known was lost. Where it exists, we do not know, although we always have envisioned it as…an enclosed green place," like a baseball diamond.

**Goodnight, Irene**

*Goodnight, Irene*: A popular American hit from the 1930s on, first recorded by "Lead Belly" Ledbetter in 1932. The lyrics sing of lost love, fantasy, and what the lyrics refer to as the "great notion" of death by drowning.

*Esso*: The international trade name for ExxonMobil and its related companies. The name is derived from the initials of the pre-1911 Standard Oil. In 1972, it was largely replaced in the U.S. by the *Exxon* brand.

*pseudo-Bauhaus boy's/Catholic highschool*: Chaminade High School in Mineola, founded in 1930, and run by the Society of Mary (the Marianists), a Roman Catholic order of priests and brothers.

*Rheingold*: first introduced in 1883, Rheingold was a favorite New York beer from 1950 to 1960, though it fell to the larger beer distributors in 1976. It was "guzzled regularly by a loyal cadre of workingmen who would just as soon have eaten nails as drink another beer maker's suds." Cf. New York Times (February 12, 2003).

*baracca*: The word I remember my father using, It appears to come from the Italian meaning a shack or shanty, but which he used to refer to a thick, gloppy recycled motor oil, though why he called the bottles with their pointed caps by that name I never asked him. At ten, I figured he knew the language better than I.

## Matadero, Riley & Company

*Ecce Homo: Behold the man*. Pilate's words to the frenzied crowd gathered in Jerusalem in preparation for the high holidays, as he showed them the beaten, scourged figure from Nazareth, after the palace soldiers had finished with him.

## Study in Black & White, 1954

*The Amboy Dukes*: a novel by Irving Schulman, first published in 1946. By the mid-1950s this pulp fiction classic had sold millions of copies. During the Eisenhower era, when Uncle Miltie, *Ozzie and Harriet* and *I Remember Mama* set the bar for middle-class taste and behavior, this novel reminded young American teenagers of the psychopathic bullies who ruled the playgrounds and the streets.

*Dien Bien Phu*: The Battle of Dien Bien Phu (March–May, 1954) was the climactic battle of the first Indochina War between the French Union's Far East Expeditionary Corps and the Viet Minh communist-nationalist revolutionaries, which ended with the defeat of the French. It was the first time a non-European colonial independence movement defeated a Western power through an armed struggle. To a fourteen-year-old, it seemed a harbinger of the coming Armageddon.

*Wimpy and Olive*: Characters featured in *Popeye the Sailor*, a cartoon strip created by Elzie Crisler Segar and continued into the 1940s and '50s by Segar's assistant, Bud Sagendorf. Butch had these small pornographic comic books which used comic characters like Cinderella and Mickey Mouse and Popeye to tell their stories.

## The Sweater

*Charlton (Moses) Heston*: Cecil B. DeMille's epic four-hour *The Ten Commandments*, which was released in 1956 and which starred Charlton Heston as Moses leading his people out of slavery, and the recalcitrant Yul Brynner as Rameses II, Pharaoh of Egypt. In 1957, it took in $185,000,000, or $1,000,000,000 in today's dollars.

## The Girl Who Learned to Sing in Crow

*nature/morte*: French for "still life." An image depicting inanimate objects; a still life. The French means, literally, "nature dead," as in an image or tableau where the life has been removed.

## Work

*Sunt lacrimae rerum*: "There are tears for such things." The Aeneid, Book I, l. 462, such things being the common fate of humankind.

## Winter 1956

Stone bridge at Andau: The Hungarian Uprising of 1956 lasted from October 23 until November 10. It began as a student demonstration began in Budapest and quickly spread across Hungary, toppling the government. On November 4th, Soviet forces invaded the country. In the next six days some 2,500 Hungarians and 700 Soviet troops were killed, and over 200,000 Hungarians fled the country. Hundreds were hunted down and executed. Within six weeks, the new Soviet-installed government was firmly in control of the country.

and shortly after the era of Joseph Stalin.


**Soldiers of Christ**

*Brando*: Marlon Brando, Jr. (1924–2004), one of the most important actors in modern American Cinema. He played a rebel motorcycle gang leader in *The Wild One* (1953), his image becoming an icon for the Blackboard Jungle pop culture of the 1950s.


**A&P Nightshift: January 1959**

*Castro and Havana*: On January 8, 1959, a week after the U.S.-backed dictator, Fulgencio Batista fled the country, the 32-year-old lawyer and revolutionary, Fidel Castro, and his 26 July Army entered Havana, thus establishing Cuba as the first Communist state in the western hemisphere.


*Joe Louis and Schmeling*: A boxing re-match between the African-American Joe Louis and the German Max Schmeling on June 22, 1938, two years after Louis lost to Schmeling in the twelfth round. The fight, which attracted more than 70,000 fans, was held at New York's Yankee Stadium in New York City. This time Louis decided to get the fight over with quickly. Ninety seconds into the fight, Louis had already hit Schmeling with a barrage of five left hooks and a body blow to his left side. Two minutes and four seconds into the first round Schmeling had gone down three times with blows to the head and the fight was over.


**Light Streaming into the Head**

*Last Judgment at Autun*: The magnificent Romanesque stone sculpture by Giselbertus on the west tympanum of the cathedral (1130–1135), depicting Christ and the Last Judgment.


*Eurydice*: Cf. Book X of Ovid's *Metamorphoses* for the story of Orpheus and Eurydice. Allen Mandelbaum translates the passage as follows:

*They'd almost reached the upper world, when he,*
*afraid that she might disappear again*
*and longing so to see her, turned to gaze back*
*at his wife. At once she slipped away—*
*and down. His arms stretched out convulsively*
*to clasp and be clasped in turn, but there*
*was nothing but the unresisting air.*

### Harry

*Remagen*: The Ludendorff Bridge at Remagen, the last bridge still standing on
the Rhine River, was captured by American troops on March 7, 1945. Although
only a limited number of forces were able to cross the Rhine before the bridge
collapsed, the Allies were able to establish a significant bridgehead on the east
side of the river.

### Crossing Cocytus

*Cocytus*: River of Lamentation in Greek mythology. The lowest of the five rivers
which encircle Dante's Hell. Dante makes of it a frozen lake, which he and Virgil
must cross over before they can leave hell behind and begin the Way of
Purgation. The source of all five rivers originates in the fall of mankind. Dante
describes Cocytus as being the home of traitors and those who committed acts of
complex fraud. Here those who betrayed family, friends, guests, country, or
one's benefactor remain eternally buried in ice.

*Yalu*: The border between China and North Korea. Thousands of Chinese
Communist troops crossed into North Korea to fight American and U.N. forces.
One memory of this that I remember as an eleven-year-old from those who wit-
nessed it is of vastly superior numbers of Chinese forces attacking American
lines in bitter cold weather, with American soldiers being overrun and killed as
their rifles and machineguns jammed.

*Belsen*: Bergen-Belsen, a Nazi P.O.W. camp in northwestern Germany, which
became a concentration camp in 1943 on the orders of Heinrich Himmler, where

Jewish hostages were held with the intention of exchanging them for German POWs. Between 1943 and the camp's liberation by the British 11th Armoured Division on April 15, 1945, an estimated 100,000 prisoners, including some 50,000 Russian soldiers, died there, many of typhus. The British found 60,000 prisoners inside, most of them seriously ill, along with 13,000 unburied corpses.

*Joe Palooka, Knobby Walsh*: Joe Palooka, American comic strip about a good-hearted, upright, and decent heavyweight boxing champion, created by cartoonist Ham Fisher in 1921. By the late 1940s, Joe Palooka was among the most popular comic strips in the country and popular as well abroad. Palooka continued to morph as new boxing champs emerged, though he always remained white, even after Joe Louis took the title. Knobby Walsh, Palooka's manager, began as a black man, but morphed into a white man sometime in the '30s. Fisher committed suicide in 1955, but the strip continued until late 1984. After a hiatus of nearly twenty-eight years, it is being revived, with Joe Palooka as a martial arts master with a golden heart. A palooka is probably derived from the derisive term, "Polack," and from about 1920 meant an inept boxer.

*Stepin Fetchit*: (1902–1985), stage name of the Black American comedian and film actor Lincoln Perry, and a contraction for "step and fetch it." Perry parlayed his talents into the stereotypic (and subversive) "Laziest Man in the World," though in reality he was highly literate and a writer for *The Chicago Defender*. The Stepin Fetchit character is rarely shown now, but in the mid-1950s it was one of my father's favorite epithets for his oldest son, whenever he didn't move fast enough to earn his $12 a week salary as a dishwasher in Baumann's Day Camp.

*Katzenjammer Kids*: American comic strip created by the German immigrant Rudolph Dirks and drawn by Harold H. Knerr from 1912 to 1949, featuring the Captain and the tykish twins, Hans and Fritz, who are continually rebelling against authority, especially their Mama, der Captain, a shipwrecked sailor who serves as surrogate father, der Inspector, an official from the school system, and the black King Bongo, who rules over a tropical island. Katzenjammer means caterwauling, or acting contritely following a hangover. In almost every episode Hans and Fritz are soundly spanked or otherwise beaten for their misdeeds.

*Batman & the Japs*: During World War II, Batman and his sidekick, Robin, were enlisted by their comic book creator to fight the Japanese, who, like Black Americans, were heavily stereotyped to the point of dehumanization.

*dank trench*: a mixture of Dante's malebolges and WWI trenches.

### Coda: Revising History

*Hawaiian Gold*: Slang for a particular species of cannabis.

*Mobil horse*: Mobil Gasoline Sign featuring a flying Red Horse, derived from the classical Greek figure of Pegasus , a white, winged divine horse, the offspring of a unicorn and a bird. Symbol of poetic inspiration.

### Ghost

his two kids/ snaking over his tattooed arms: Cf. *The Aeneid*, Book II, and the episode of the two giant serpents who rise up out of the sea to kill the Trojan priest Laocoön and his two sons.

*White Rose*: a Scotch whiskey.

### Quid Pro Quo

*Quid Pro Quo*: Latin: this for that, tit for tat. An equal exchange or substitution of goods or services.

*Vanni Fucci's figs*: Cf. Dante's *Inferno*, XXIV, 97–111. Vanni Fucci, a man "of blood and anger," who makes the sign of the fig—meaning "screw you"—to the Divine Creator by placing his thumb between the forefinger and middle finger of each hand.

*Confessions and Summa*: The *Confessions* of St. Augustine, and the *Summa Theologica* of St. Thomas Aquinas.

### Eurydice

*Agent Orange*: code name for one of the defoliants used by the U.S. military as part of its herbicidal warfare program during the Vietnam War from 1961 to 1971. Manufactured for the U.S. Department of Defense, it was later discovered to be contaminated with 2,3,7,8-tetrachlorodibenzodioxin, an extremely toxic dioxin compound. Vietnam estimates 400,000 people were killed or maimed, and 500,000 children born with birth defects as a result of the defoliant.

*some operatic scene by Gluck: Orfeo ed Euridice*, opera composed by Christoph Willibald Gluck based on the myth of Orpheus and first performed at Vienna in 1762. On the way out of Hades, Eurydice is delighted to be returning to earth, but the stoic Orpheus refuses to look at her or explain himself. She does not understand his action and reproaches him, but he must suffer in silence. When Eurydice chides him for what she takes to be his coldness, Orpheus turns to her and she disappears, returning to Hell.

**The Dancing Master**

*Dante's line splits into Baudelaire's/polis*: When I began my doctoral studies in English and Comparative Literature at the newly-formed Graduate Center of the City University of New York, I didn't have a clue. It was Allen Mandelbaum, then in his late thirties, who took me under his wing and guided me, making statements such as those mentioned in this poem. It was a class in Dante, but Allen brought in everything, such as this statement about the modern city— Dante's Florence, Baudelaire's Paris, and Eliot's London, to which I would in time add Williams's Paterson, Lowell's Boston, Berryman's Minneapolis and St. Paul, Hart Crane's Cleveland and New York, Hopkins' Dublin, and Stevens' Hartford, among others.

*Francesco's hermitage*: the grotto of St. Francis of Assisi. Though it is now forty-two years on, the image of Allen meditating in the stone chapel alone as the rest of us came up on him remains vivid in my mind. "His true calling on earth was his poetic mission." His son, Jonathan, said, following his father's death in 2011. "He had spent his life preparing for the ultimate journey. All the master-pieces of classical and medieval literature that he translated were, in a sense, chronicles of immense journeys. That near-obsession with travel, that restless-ness, that curiosity, led him to spend more time and effort translating the works of other faiths, even as he remained true to his Jewish roots."

**The Old Men are Dying**

*Calvary*: The Roman Catholic Cemetery on Laurel Hill Blvd. in Woodside, Queens. Begun in 1817, when space in Manhattan began to give out, it is a veritable city of the dead, with a population of more than 3 million.

**The Statue**

*venti anni fa*: Italian for "twenty years ago."

*Venti settembre*: Italian for September 20th (1870), the day Rome was annexed to the Kingdom of Italy, ending the temporal power of the Popes. Streets all over Italy bear this name.

*Sulmona*: Ovid was born in this town on the spine of the Abruzzi mountains. His statue dominates the town square. It was the first inkling I had that my mentor, the indefatigable Allen Mandelbaum, was already planning to translate Ovid's *Metamorphoses*, once he had completed his translations of Virgil, Dante, Ungaretti, Quasimodo, the Milanese poet, Giovanni Giudici, and others.

**As Mirandola Had It, The Mirror of the Soul**

*Mirandola*: Count Giovanni Pico della Mirandola (1463–1494), the Italian Renaissance philosopher. At 23, he wrote his Oration on the Dignity of Man. Along with other Renaissance Neo-Platonists, he wrote that the face of the Divine is reflected in the mirror of the soul. To know oneself, therefore—that is, to come to see oneself—is to come to better know God.

*coup de grace*: French for a "blow of mercy", i.e., ending the life of a wounded creature with a blow or gunshot to the head, without the consent of the sufferer. The sense of grace here is of course used ironically. Back some thirty years ago, I was giving a series of readings in central Georgia and had the opportunity to visit Flannery O'Connor's farm, Andalusia, on the outskirts of Milledgeville. Something of the mysterious beauty and sublime terror of Flannery's world struck me on that visit to the south, which I am still grappling with.

**For the Union Dead at Andersonville**

*Andersonville*: Confederate prison, in operation from February 1864 until April 1865. By August 1864 there were over 33,000 prisoners crammed into the camp's 26 acres. Some 13,000 Union prisoners died there of malnutrition, exposure, and disease during that time.

**On the Sublime**

*Burke*: Edmund Burke, British statesman and philosopher (1729–1797). In his treatise on The Sublime and the Beautiful, written in the wake of the French Reign of Terror, he explains that whatever gives rise to terror in the soul is a source of the sublime, the strongest emotion we can feel. "When danger or pain press too nearly," he notes, "they are incapable of giving any delight, and are simply terrible; but at certain distances, and with certain modifications, they may be, and they are, delightful, as we every day experience."

*Longinus*: name given to the author of the treatise, *On the Sublime*, a treatise on aesthetics and a work of literary criticism. To be a truly great writer, Longinus advises, one must elevate one's style with "great thoughts, strong emotions, certain figures of thought and speech, noble diction, and dignified word arrangement". The purpose of the Sublime for him was to literally take readers outside of themselves (exstasis). Among examples of the Sublime he names Homer, Sophocles, Sappho, Plato, Genesis, even Aristophanes for his mordant humor which cut through the surface of things to a deeper truth.

*Turner*: J. M. W. Turner (1775–1851), the English Romantic landscape painter. On October 16, 1834, the Palace of Westminster was destroyed by a huge conflagration, the largest to strike London since the Great fire of 1666, and attracted massive crowds. One of those who witnessed the fire at first hand was Turner himself.

**On the Limits of Transcendence**

*Romanenko*: Yury Romanenko (b. 1944), Russian astronaut. His first flight was on December 10, 1977 on Soyuz 26 to the space station Salyut 6. He spent 96 days in space. Ten years later, he flew out to the Mir space station, where he lived for the next 326 days and conducted three space walks. On December 29, 1987 he returned to earth.

*William Carlos Williams*: Cf. Williams's late poem, "Heel and Toe to the End," celebrating Yuri Gagarin's flight into space in 1961. Gagarin (1934–1968), a Soviet pilot and cosmonaut, was the first human to journey into outer space, when his Vostok spacecraft completed a single orbit of the Earth on April 12, 1961. It was his only space flight. He died in 1968 when the MiG jet he was flying crashed. Williams's poem begins: "Gagarin says, in ecstasy, / he could have/ gone on forever."

*Mayakovsky*: Vladimir Mayakovsky (1893–1930), Russian revolutionary poet and playwright. Williams met Mayakovsky at Lola Ridge's salon apartment in Greenwich Village in the 1920s, and remarked that Mayakovsky's recitation of his poems in his native Russian felt to him as if Homer were in the room reciting *The Iliad*.

### Sarcophagus
*Masaccio*: Masaccio (1401–1428), born Tommaso di Ser Giovanni di Simone, the first great painter of the Italian Quattrocento. The Expulsion from the Garden of Eden is a fresco from the cycle painted ca. 1425 by Masaccio in the Brancacci Chapel of Santa Maria del Carmine in Florence.

### The Eastern Point Meditations
*Merton*: Thomas Merton, O.C.S.O. (1915–1968), the Anglo-American Catholic writer and mystic and a Trappist monk of the Abbey of Gethsemani, Kentucky, from 1941 until his death. In Ceylon a week before his death by accidental electrocution, Merton visited the huge stone statues of the Buddha at Polannaruwa. In that sacred space, he wrote, "I don't know when in my life I have ever had such a sense of beauty and spiritual validity running together in one aesthetic illumination. ...I mean I know and have seen what I was obscurely looking for. I don't know what else remains but I have now seen and pierced through the surface and have got beyond the shadow and the disguise."

*Kurosawa's bandits*: Cf. *The Seven Samurai*, by the Japanese director, Akiri Kurosawa (1910–1996). One of the greatest films ever made, it was released in 1954, nine years after the end of WWII. The film takes place in 1587 during a period of great internal struggle in Japan, and follows the story of a village of farmers who hire seven samurai to combat a group of ruthless bandits who mean to return after the harvest to steal the farmers' crops.

*Nuntius*: Latin for messenger or message. Cf. by extension, nuncio, as in Papal Nuncio, or ambassador.

*Pan dolce*: From the Ligurian region of Italy. A nut cake with dried fruits.

*Our Lady of Good Voyage*: The Roman Catholic church in Gloucester built by the Portuguese community and dedicated to the Blessed Mother. A statue of Our Lady of Good Voyage holds the Christ child in her left arm, and a fishing boat in her right as a symbol of a safe voyage. As a young man, T.S. Eliot spent his summers in Gloucester. In the fourth part of *Dry Salvages*, he invokes Our Lady of Good Voyage: "Lady, whose shrine stands on the promontory,/Pray for all those who are in ship" as well as those who

> Ended their voyage on the sand, in the sea's lips
> Or in the dark throat which will not reject them
> Or wherever cannot reach them the sounds of the sea bell's
> Perpetual angelus.

### Giottoesque: Christmas 1985

*Gander*: Gander Air Force Base, Newfoundland. On the morning of December 12, 1985, a Douglas DC-8 jetliner, carrying U.S. troops from Cairo, Egypt, to their home base in Fort Campbell, Kentucky, via Cologne, Germany and Gander, crashed shortly after takeoff and burned about half a mile from the runway, killing all 256 passengers and crew on board.

*Halley's Comet*: A comet visible to the naked eye from Earth every 75 years. It has been observed and recorded since about 240 BCE by Chinese, Babylonian, and medieval European chroniclers, though the fact that this was the same comet returning was only determined by the English astronomer Edmond Halley in 1705, and for which it is named. It appeared in 1985/6. Look for it again in 2061.

*Giotto*: both the Trecento painter Giotto di Bondone and a European robotic spacecraft mission from the European Space Agency, intended to fly by and study Halley's Comet. On 13 March 1986, Giotto came within 350 miles of the comet's nucleus. Giotto observed the comet in 1301 and depicted it as the star of Bethlehem in his *Adoration of the Magi*.

### The Cistern

*I am a man gone down into the pit*: Cf. Psalm 88, a poem Christ may well have recited to himself in the cistern as he waited for his trial that Good Friday morning. We do know that he recited other Psalms from the cross, which were misheard or misread by the authorities.

### Death & Transfiguration

*Church/of the Transfiguration*: Part of a Franciscan monastery complex on Mount Tabor in Israel, designed by Antonio Barluzzi and completed in 1924. The Art Deco-styled church was built on the ruins of an ancient Byzantine church, which had been followed by a 12th century Crusader church. It is the site where the Transfiguration of Christ is believed to have taken place, where Jesus was transfigured and spoke with Moses and Elijah (the Law and the Prophets). *Fratelli*: the brothers.

*Raphael*: the great High Renaissance master (1483–1520). *The Transfiguration* is considered the artist's last painting, now housed in the Pinacoteca Vaticana. Commissioned by Cardinal Giulio de Medici, who later became Pope Clement VII. Rather than send the painting to France, the cardinal donated it to the church of San Pietro in Montorio in Rome.

*a light like ten thousand suns that flames the brain*: Ironically, August 6th commemorates two events: the Feast of the Transfiguration of Christ, and the dropping of the Atomic Bomb on a Japanese city, Hiroshima, on August 6, 1945.

### Fear

*Wild Bill*: The poet William Matthews (1942–1997), wit, raconteur, poet, friend, translator of Horace and Martial, avid basketball fan, opera devotee, and Jazz aficionado.

*Bird*: Larry Bird, star player for the Boston Celtics from 1979 until his retirement in 1992.

*Mingus*: Charles Mingus Jr. (1922–1979), the American jazz musician, composer, whom Matthews recalled in both his poems and in his conversations.

### Voyager

*Voyager*: space probe launched by NASA in 1977, to study the outer solar system and interstellar space. Now somewhere in deep space, it is the farthest man-made object sent out from Earth, and will most likely be the first probe to leave the Solar System altogether.

### Silt

St. Bernard: Cf. Canto XXXIII of the *Paradiso*.

### North/South

*Pas de deux*: a dance for two, consisting of entrée and adagio, a variation for each dancer, and a coda; a close relationship between two people or things, as during an activity.

### Shadow of the Father

*Protoevangelium*: The Gospel of James, an apocryphal Gospel probably written about AD 145, which expands upon the infancy stories in Matthew and Luke, and presents a narrative concerning the birth and upbringing of Mary herself.

**The Fathers**

*Cri de coeur*: French. A passionate outcry of appeal or protest, used here ironically.

*Palestinian gunmen*: The Siege of the Church of the Nativity in Bethlehem, April 2nd to May 10th, 2002 by Palestinian extremists. Israel Defense Forces responded by occupying the town and trying to capture the militants, many of whom fled into the Church of the Nativity to seek refuge. Finally, after nearly forty days, the militants turned themselves in to Israel and were exiled to Europe and the Gaza Strip.

**They Shall Beat Their Swords**

*Abbottabad*: On Monday, May 2, 2011, shortly after 1:00a.m., Osama bin Laden, former head of the Islamist militant group al-Qaeda, was killed at his compound in Abbottabad, Pakistan by United States Navy SEALs, by order of President Barack Obama . Bin Laden's body was then flown to Afghanistan for identification, before being buried at sea, within 24 hours of his death.

**The Gift**

*Stay, thou art so fair*:  Cf. Goethe's *Faust*:

*If to the moment I shall ever say:*
*"Ah, stay, thou art so fair!"*
*Then may you fetters on me lay,*
*Then will I perish, then and there!*

With  these words the Romantic overreacher Faust seals his bargain with the devil, who can then claim Faust's soul. Faust believes what many young romantics believe: that he shall always search and never be satisfied with any earthly moment. But that is before love enters the picture.

**When We Walked Together**

*In the cool of the evening*: Cf. Genesis 3:8.

*A number of the poems included here carry dedications, though many others are clearly dedicated to the individuals celebrated in the poems themselves.*

*Mairsy Doats*: for my father, Paul, and my uncle and godfather, Louis Mariani
*East of the Whitestone*: for my oldest friend, Bob Sandroni
*Soldiers of Christ*: for Ron Hansen
*A&P Nightshift*: for Phil Levine, collaborator and friend
*Manhattan*: for Bob Creeley (1926–2005)
*Coda: Revising History*: for my brother, Walter
*The Republic*: for Frank Serpico and the memory of David Ignatow (1914–1997)
*The Dancing Master*: to the sacred memory of Allen Mandelbaum (1926–2011)
*Early Autumn Song*: for Cathy O'Connell
*The Statue*: to the sacred memory of Allen Mandelbaum
*As Mirandola Had It*: to the sacred memory of Flannery O'Connor (1925–1964)
*On the Sublime*: for Terrence Des Pres (1939–1987)
*On the Limits of Transcendence*: for Terrence Des Pres (1939–1987)
*Giottoesque*: for Margaret & Jim Freeman
*The Gods Who Come Among Us*: for Charlie Miller
*Pietà*: for Fr. Warren Savage
*The Great Wheel*: for Ed Callahan (1939–1992)
*Fear*: for Bill Matthews (1943–1996)
*Variations on a Theme*: for Donald Justice (1925–2004)
*The Blank Canvas*: for James Franco
*Words*: for Barry Moser, collaborator and friend
*The Things They Taught Me*: for those I was fortunate enough to teach over the
        past four decades
*North/South*: for Bob Pack, collaborator and friend
*Light*: for my community at Bread Loaf
*Passage*: to the sacred memory of Mary & Phil Spinosa
*Hopkins in Ireland*: for the Jesuit Community at Boston College
*The Fathers*: for Fr. Bill McNichols
*Sestina*: for Peggy Parker & the community at Orvieto
*Putting Out in the Deep*: for Fr. Harry Cain & Ginny Blass, Eastern Point,
        August 8, 2011

Many of these poems have appeared, most in earlier versions, in the following periodicals and quarterlies, to whose editors grateful acknowledgment is made here: *Agni Review, America Magazine, The Best Catholic Writing, Boston College Magazine, Crazyhorse, Doubletake, The Flannery O'Connor Review, The Gettysburg Review, Image Journal, The Kenyon Review, The New Criterion, The New England Review/Bread Loaf Quarterly, Pleiades, Ploughshares, Poetry* (Chicago), *Prairie Schooner, Quarterly West, Sewanee Theological Review, Spiritual Life, The Tampa Review, Triquarterly Review, Vineyards.* The author would also like to thank those who in various ways (sometimes unbeknown to them) helped shape this volume, some thirty-seven years in the making. Among these are: Michael Astrue, Robert Bagg, Jill Bialosky, Ben Birnbaum, Harold Bloom, J.D. Bottums, Scott Cairns, Kate Daniels, Terrence Des Pres, Vincent DiMarco, Brian Doyle, Sharon Dunn, Martin Espada, Pete Fairchild, Harold Fickett, Adam Fitzgerald, James Franco, Andrew Frisardi, Daniela Gioseffi, Giovanni Giudici, David Godine, Tom Grady, Ron Hansen, Michael Harper, Seamus Heaney, Bill Heyen, Edward Hirsch, Mark Jarman, Donald Junkins, Philip Kolin, Andrew Krivak, Julius Lester, Philip Levine, John Mahoney, Allen Mandelbaum, James Martin, s.j., Don Martin, Valerie Martin, Suzanne Matson, Bill Matthews, John Montague, Barry Moser, Angela Alaimo O'Donnell, Robert Pack, Linda Pastan, Wyatt Prunty, Steven Schoenberg, Peter Stitt, James Tate, James Torrens, s.j., Ellen Bryant Voigt, Richard Wilbur, Greg Wolfe, and the folks at Wipf & Stock. And then, of course, there is my extended family, among them my wife and sons, Paul and Mark and John, as well as my parents and grandparents and grandchildren, who are at the heart of so many of these poems.

*Paul Mariani's*

EPITAPHS FOR THE JOURNEY

*was designed by Barry Moser who also drew and engraved the*

*images on the book's jacket and facing the title page. The Alpha and*

*Omega devices are from* TIMING DEVICES, *Mariani's first book*

*of poems that was published in 1977 by the Pennyroyal Press.*

*It too was designed and illustrated by Mr Moser*

*who engraved the Alpha and Omega devices herein*

*for that publication.*

*The type used in both books is Herman Zapf's enduring Palatino,*

*originally issued in 1948 by the Linotype Corporation.*

*The cutting used in this volume is from*

*the Adobe Corporation issued in 1991.*

*The typeface is named after the sixteenth century Italian*

*calligrapher Giambattista Palatino whose work informed Zapf's*

*designs. It was composed in QuarkXpress 6.1.*

*by the designer.*

*http://moser-pennyroyal.com*